Noblesse Oblige

THE DUCHESS OF WINDSOR AS I KNEW HER

To Cindy:

I regret I did not meet you
when I was fortunate to meet
Aida.
Sincerely
René
June 2012

RICHARD RENÉ SILVIN

Front cover photo by Maximilian Kaufmann, The Photography Studio, Inc., West Palm Beach, Florida

Front cover picture insert of *Time Magazine* shows Wallis Simpson, later the Duchess of Windsor, named as "Person of the Year" for 1936, the first time the magazine gave a woman this title.

Time rather awkwardly explained the distinction as follows:

"In the single year 1936 she became the most-talked-about, written about, headlined and interest-compelling person in the world. In these respects no woman in history has equaled Mrs. Simpson, for no press or radio existed to spread the world news they made."

Editing of this manuscript by Nicole Musick

This book is based on some true events, however, has been fictionalized and all persons appearing in this work are fictitious. Any resemblance to real people, living or dead, is entirely coincidental.

ISBN: 0-615-50578-3
ISBN-13: 978-0-615-50578-7

INDEX

Part One

YOUNG UPSTART

Chapter 1

The Duchess was late, which was most unusual. For social events she was deliberately tardy, but definitely not for her business meetings. Her heightened sense of duty and purpose forbade being late – cold, combative, sometimes amusing or sarcastic, often aloof but not late *and* she had agreed to attend today's meeting in order to help me.

Wallis, Duchess of Windsor, was preoccupied; some said befuddled. She had recently undergone a hip replacement operation and detested using her "walking stick." She was also newly widowed, a state she found to be very difficult. Her late husband, former King Edward VIII of England, had died of cancer in May of 1972, after thirty-six years of marriage. Wallis was also anxious about concluding an agreement with the French authorities to donate all of her Louis Seize antiques to the French government for display at Versailles and the Louvre.

I suppose, at seventy eight years of age, she was both contemplating her famous and notorious life as well as her death - which would not occur until April 24, 1986. In spite of three marriages, the Duchess had no children. Both she and the late Duke of Windsor, as he was called after he abdicated the British throne in order to marry her, were

3

estranged from their very different families. There was, of course, abundant buzz about which charity would receive the bulk of their wealth upon her death. The International Hospital of Paris was the most widely rumored potential beneficiary of her estate. Wallis had been the subject of such speculation and gossip for forty years, yet was not immune to its effects. "I despise people's ignorant theories about me," she said to me on more than one occasion.

There were several reasons why the idea of The International Hospital being the primary beneficiary of the Duchess's estate appeared logical. As residents of France for several decades, both the Duke and Duchess were treated at the world renowned hospital with growing frequency. Following the Duke's death, the Duchess had agreed to serve as an honorary member of the hospital's Board of Governors; the type of task she was not used to accepting lightly and which did not go unnoticed when she joined the Board. Finally, a magnificent estate located near Cannes, France had been auctioned as its owner's will had required. All proceeds of the sale went to the International Hospital. Clearly, numerous Board members hoped that the Duchess' estate would also eventually subsidize the mounting operational losses at the hospital.

In an article the Duchess had allowed to be published in August of 1973 she wrote:

"Although the Duke and I decided long ago to make our home in France, I regularly spend part of each year in the United States, and I remain an American citizen. Since 1972 I have been privileged to serve as an Honorary Governor of the International Hospital of Paris. This is an institution I have come to admire, for it is a unique ambassador of goodwill for the United States."

The hospital was located in the fashionable Parisian suburb of Neuilly-Sur-Seine, not far from her home on the Route du Champ d'Entrainement. The previous occupant of the Royal couple's home was General and Mrs. Charles de Gaulle. Many years later, the grand home was leased from the city of Paris by Mohamed Al Fayed. Some say it was the destination of Princess Diana and her reckless lover, Dody Al Fayed, the night they were tragically killed while racing away from the paparazzi; driven by a drunken chauffeur. Ironically, the Duchess was probably the first celebrity ever to be chased by the paparazzi in 1936 when she "escaped" from England. Mohamed Al Fayed maintains the home exactly as it was during Wallis' last years. While Wallis did donate some antiques to different museums, the beautiful ninetieth century estate remains almost exactly as the Duchess left it when she died. In the leaseholder's words, "it is as if the Duke and Duchess had just gone out to dinner."

Thinking of the Duchess, I, again, glanced at my watch.

"I suggest we begin the meeting," The debonair Honorable Perry Culley, the Board's President, said.

"Well this proves she *does* have balls," said Gregory O'Neal, the founder and head of the American Chamber of Commerce in Paris. His rough words were as harsh as his appearance. He was referring to one of the hundreds of rumors about the famous lady. A particularly cruel, and false, anecdote asserted that the Duchess suffered from "testicular feminism" and *actually* had glands resembling testicles.

"That story was pretty well discarded after the Duchess's cancer operation and her hip replacement here a few months ago, wouldn't you agree?" answered Ted Williams, the US Ambassador to OECD, the Organization for Economic Cooperation and Development. Mr.

Williams was also a professional board member who served on the boards of AT&T, General Electric and IBM. Many of the "personages," in the Franco-American high society community living in Paris were directly connected to IBM and its founders: the Watson family.

"She rarely comes to these meetings because we refuse to call her 'Your Royal Highness,'" said Pierre Redhouse, Chief Executive Officer of all IBM operations in Europe and the Middle East.

"I doubt that is the reason," I interjected as respectfully as possible. "Few honorary members attend our meetings and we have listed her on all our information as 'H.R.H. the Duchess of Windsor.'" Redhouse was referring to the "insult" that both the Duke and Duchess never overcame. On the eve of their June 3, 1937 wedding in France, word came from Buckingham Palace that Wallis would never be allowed to be referred to as "HRH" and called "Your Royal Highness." Such a title requires all women to curtsy and men to bow in their presence. The malicious decision was without legal precedence and was largely disregarded by both the Duke and Wallis.

"You said The Duchess would be here," barked Chairman Otto Passman at me.

Passman was not the Chairman of the hospital but rather the Chairman of the powerful Foreign Operations Subcommittee on Appropriations of the US House of Representatives. For very different reasons he, like I, was an invited guest to the regular Board meetings. Chairman Passman attended because he loved a reason to come to Paris and, hypocritically, we pretended to love indulging his every wish and need. I, as acting hospital administrator, hired by USAID, a division of The State Department, was the other non-member of this august gathering allowed to attend meetings. I was the young-

6

est participant by several decades. Under their watchful eyes, I would deliver a summary of the major events occurring at the hospital, the progress of the plans to build a replacement facility and a report on the current famous patients we were treating, or scheduled to treat, as they flew in, some on their private aircraft long before such travel habits were common.

Things had not been going well for me as the hospital director and The Duchess, along with Perry Culley and General Solberg, were my only vocal supporters. Her absence today would be a disappointment to the other board members who regaled in seeing her and bringing details of her appearance and comments back to other socialites in Paris. I was not concerned about cocktail party gossip but rather in keeping my job as it was under attack by the hospital's Chief of Staff, Doctor Sheldon Cheek, a new Board member. The Duchesses' absence could well mean the difference between receiving a severe reprimand, at the very least, and being allowed free passage to continue my work.

Fortunately, the uncomfortable chatter was silenced by the sirens of the police car which would often lead The Duchess' chauffer driven limousine around Paris; a courtesy extended to the Duchess after she was widowed. The Board members, all men of course, tightened their ties and straightened their jackets. Practically everyone groveled and forced themselves forward to bow, kissed her hand and offered a few polite yet insincere words of praise. As Lady Diana Cooper said, "People sharpened up when The Duchess entered a room." Today was certainly no exception.

Regardless of how severe the criticism was of the iconic woman, no one could responsibly denigrate her appearance and style. She had what the French call "allure" and seemed to have coined the phrase "you cannot be too rich or too thin." She always looked both very rich and very thin. She was frequently rated number one on the world's "ten best dressed list." Today her immaculate dark hair was, as usual, parted in the middle and pulled back into a small, tidy bun. She was wearing a well tailored dark blue suit with white trim. When a friend told Wallis that she never saw her wear the same dress twice, Wallis replied, "But my dear, how is that possible? I only order one hundred dresses a year."

For her appearance at today's meeting she looked as fit and fashionable as usual, but she also commanded the impression of someone on a professional mission.

As we all progressed toward our usual places at the large table located in a villa adjacent to the main hospital building, she beckoned me over, "I hope you know that Cheek over there has lobbied all his wealthy American widow friends and is expressing his outrage over you, René," she said. "You have hit a nerve with these new reports you initiated. It's rather fascinating really," she concluded and winked with an almost wicked smile. "I'd like to hear more about it. He refers to you as the 'young upstart' you know." The three decades of marriage to "David" as she, his family and all close friends affectionately called Edward had bred a slight British accent. Her strong voice was also unique and her diction was an interesting mix of a southern drawl and the honestly acquired British accent.

"Yes Duchess," I responded trying to conceal my concern. "I know what he calls me and the matter *is* on the agenda."

"Just stay calm. He is a pompous and arrogant man. How it is that he manages to influence some of my friends is amazing to me. It is because of this little matter that I came here today. God knows I can appreciate being the victim of a plot! You have nothing to worry about and we will laugh about this over dinner at Maxim's (spelled Maxime, in French) one evening soon, you'll see. It may be hard for you to understand right now but this will be a positive in your life and I will enjoy what I am about to do."

"Thank you, Duchess," I said.

"Noblesse Oblige, René. I am here to do my bit for you," she said using one of her favorite expressions.

Our discussion was abbreviated by the meeting being called to order.

But first, I need to explain how I became the "young upstart," how a simple girl from Baltimore became The Duchess of Windsor and how the man who was groomed to be – indeed **was** – King of England ended up as a "mere" Duke – albeit arguably the most famous of all Dukes in history.

In time, I would learn that history's rather brutal portrayal of the Duchess was unfair and unwarranted. She was not a calculating, self-centered and manipulating woman but rather a brilliant planner and fun-loving eccentric who, when necessary, viciously protected her loved ones.

The Duchess of Windsor 1974 with Princess Margret and her husband the Earl of Snowden at the Waldorf Towers in New York.

The Princess' divorce in 1979 is the worst Royal scandal since the abdication.

Chapter 2

THE EARLY DAYS (1896 – 1929)
WALLIS

Bessie Wallis Warfield was most likely born on June 19, 1896 in Blue Ridge Summit, Pennsylvania. No birth certificate was issued, so the exact year is a matter of some debate as is the question of when her parents were married. Her mother, Alice (sometimes spelled Alys) Montague was from a well to do family in Baltimore, Maryland. However, the young family did not live at the Montague house; some speculate because Wallis' parents were not married at the time of her conception. Her infancy was mostly spent with her mother and her aunt, Bessie Merryman. It was not a life of luxury. The result of these early years would mark Wallis for life and would create, in her, a desire for perfection in décor, clothing, and impeccably prepared and served dinners. The baby girl was not baptized and would not be confirmed until she was fifteen. Eventually her baptismal and birth records were falsified, to look more "proper," so that she could marry, Edward, who among other titles was the former "keeper of the faith" of the Church of England.

Shortly after her birth, mother and child lived with Wallis' father, Teackle Warfield, who was seriously ill with "consumption" or tuberculosis. Given what was known about the disease in those days, her father was never allowed to hug or kiss his baby daughter. He died in 1897 at the age of twenty-six; Wallis was probably one.

Alice and her sister, Bessie, worshipped the precautious and roguish little Wallis. They showered her with love and affection and did their best to fulfill the child's every need. "Aunt Bessie" would remain a close family member and advisor throughout Wallis' life, whereas her mother, Alice, died in 1929 shortly before her daughter became an international celebrity. As early as her mid teens Wallis, like many young women of the period, had a serious crush on Prince Edward of England, the future Prince of Wales and presumably, the future King of England and Emperor of the British Empire.

In 1915, Wallis met a debonair young navy pilot named Earl Winfield (Win) Spencer who she married in November, 1916. The young couple's honeymoon, both literal and figurative, was short. Win was getting ready to go to war and he drank to excess. There is abundant speculation that he was bisexual and, perhaps, dealt with his concealed sexual desires with alcohol. Shortly after their wedding, at an air show in Pensacola, Florida, Wallis witnessed the crash and death of one of their young pilot friends. The horrible scene gave Wallis an acute fear of flying which would last for the rest of her life, during which she only flew a handful of times. One such occasion took place when they returned to New York, via airplane, following the Duke's surgery in Houston. Wallis was jittery and preoccupied, clutching her hands in a unique way which would become her signature way to handle stress. The Duke supposedly turned to Wallis and said, "Why don't you let the pilot fly the plane, darling?"

Within two years of Wallis and Win's wedding, they were both having affairs: Win with boisterous, drunken people and Wallis with men of ever increasing importance. She had a knack of studying her dates' interests and filling the conversation with her newly acquired knowledge.

Toward the end of the "war to end all wars," Wallis was drafted by Naval Intelligence for the purpose of passing secret messages to friends and allies of the United States. This was common in those days, as no form of electronic communication was "secure." Her first, brief missions were to England and France where an impressionable young Wallis saw beautifully dressed women of high society in the grand hotels of London and Paris. She became determined to one day become a part of the fashionable world of the *haute bourgeoisie*. The practice of having government, military, or royal wives pass secrets to their counterparts in foreign countries still exists in the Arab and Persian cultures.

In 1923 and 1924, shortly before the outbreak of the Chinese civil war, Wallis resided in China, again on a mission for Naval Intelligence. By means that are unclear, and would only fuel unsubstantiated rumors, it was there that she learned many advanced sexual techniques. While in China, she developed several important relationships that would last until these people died many years later. Sadly for her, Wallis outlived everyone of importance in her earlier life. One such pivotal friendship was with Katherine and Herman Rogers. Another was with an Italian diplomat, Count Galeazzo Ciano. Wallis most likely became pregnant with the Count's child and may have performed a self induced abortion which led to the hospitalization of a seriously ill Wallis at a woman's clinic. As a result, she would suffer from gynecological problems for the rest of her life and was likely incapable of conception.

Once back in the United States, her marriage worsened. In 1927, to the horror of her family, she divorced Win while living in Virginia. She then met a more "sophisticated" man by the name of Ernest Simpson who was half American and half British. Wallis wanted to marry Ernest who had served in the prestigious British Coldstream Guard. Some historian's claim that Ernest was not, as his name implies, totally honest with Wallis during their first several meetings. It is suggested that he concealed several important facts about himself including the "detail" that he was married and had a daughter. While he soon revealed this matter to Wallis, he continued to hide the fact that he was Jewish and the family had changed its name from Solomon to Simpson. After her new beaux's divorce, Wallis married him in 1928. Since Ernest's father was the senior partner in a ship brokerage company with offices in England and Germany, the newlyweds moved to London to work for the family business.

Once in England, using her proven methods of cleverly researching her targets, whether friend or lover, Wallis managed to make inroads into society. One of her friends was the wealthy Thelma, Lady Furness; the twin sister of Gloria Vanderbilt and, most importantly, Prince Edward's mistress.

Like so many women, Wallis had a nearly hysteric fascination for the handsome and beloved Prince of Wales. However, the exact date of her introduction to the Prince is unclear. Even Wallis and the Duke differed in their recollection of the month, but everyone agrees on certain details of the meeting; it took place in 1929 and was arranged by Thelma. Wallis was understandably nervous. She was suffering from a cold and was unsure of herself. There are reports that she practiced her obligatory curtsey for the Prince while on the train the same day. On either the first or second encounter, it was already clear that Wallis had understood the Prince's Achilles heel. He liked an assertive woman, not afraid to admonish him. In fact, she took the huge risk of gently, yet publically, scolding him by saying how "disappointed" she was in his "narrow view of American women" after he had made a comment about their inability to enjoy the British climate. The ploy worked as the never-criticized Prince found Wallis endearing and, eventually, fascinating.

Somehow Wallis' unprecedented admonishment endeared her to the Prince possibly because it positioned her as a strong, maternal figure. Wallis instinctively understood that the "most eligible bachelor in the world" needed and cherished a firm mother substitute. Whether or not she consciously knew that the Prince's mother, Queen Mary, was incapable of affectionate demonstrative motherly love, Wallis quickly filled a huge need in Prince Edward.

At around this time, Margaret, Duchess of Argyll described Wallis as "quite a plain woman with a noticeably square jaw, and not particularly amusing." While the Duchess of Argyll was correct about Wallis' jaw, she underestimated Wallis who was able to maximize her talents and even her faults. While never a beauty, she would, in due course, create her own immaculate, understated and timeless style of dress and make up. And, as I know firsthand, she had a well-developed, sarcastic wit, a busty sense of humor and a keen grasp of social politics. She never lost a battle she was committed to win.

Wallis Warfield circa 1920

Mrs. Simpson with her dog, Slipper 1936

EDWARD, PRINCE OF WALES

Born in June 1894, Edward Albert Christopher George Andrew Patrick David Windsor was Queen Victoria's great grandson, the son of King George V and Queen Mary. The oldest of five children, he would eventually have three brothers (George, Albert, and Henry) and a sister, Mary. Many people get confused with the fact that it was Albert, not George who became King George VI when he ascended to the throne after Edward's abdication. As most frequently is the case, Edward, the first male born to the British monarch, became the Prince of Wales and, from his earliest education, was groomed to become King. He was charming, striking, physically fit and spoiled. He wasn't tall, but had a sensitive, sweet face and a full head of healthy blonde hair and premature bags under his sad, endearing, light blue eyes. Some claimed that he was an insomniac, which irritated the Prince who even went to great lengths to rebuff the idea that he took sleeping pills during the fateful abdication week in December of 1936. Edward's passions were the study of history, international relations, travel, gardening and, of course, the British Empire which he would rule over for only three hundred twenty five days in 1936.

As the likely future ruler of one third of the globe, Prince Edward traveled extensively and set a precedence of being the only well known and recognizable member of the Royal family due to his visits to every country in the Empire. His world tours during the 1920's had made him loved by the vast majority of his future subjects and he became – by far – the most eligible bachelor in the world of the day. He was pro-labor which made him the first popular member of the Royal family among the working class. He was thought of as the "people's

Prince." In an odd way, Edward's reputation was an interesting combination of the recent, late Princess Diana *and* her son, Prince William. Princess Diana and Wallis also had two things in common: a lonely childhood devoid of friends and a great sense of style. They differed on their ability to control political crises which ultimately affected the outcome of their futures in very different ways.

The Prince particularly loved Austria and Germany and, as a result, spoke fluent German. A well concealed oddity was his probable bizarre sexual activities when, numerous accounts claim, that among other things, he imitated children during love making. He adored his mother throughout her long life and, had details been known, would be called a "momma's boy" today. This probably explains his acceptance of, even appreciation for, Wallis' famous early rebukes and her complete control over Edward after their marriage.

Within a few years of their first meeting, Wallis would become the central figure in Edward's life and one without whom he simply could not function. Even more fascinating is the fact that she could easily have remained "the royal mistress" or, under certain limited circumstances, married Edward while he was King. But Edward would tolerate no compromise and, as we will explore in more detail later, he gave up the throne to marry Wallis on his own terms. As he said: "On the Throne or not, I shall marry Mrs. Simpson."

The entire world was riveted to the rapid turn of events in the first two weeks of December 1936 as the decision to abdicate was formulated. Edward's choice to give up the crown lead to Britain's most serious constitutional crisis. In his address to the nation he said, in part, "... you must believe me when I tell you that I have found it impossible to carry the heavy burden of responsibility and to discharge my duties as King, as I wish to do, without the help and support of the woman I love…." In an attempt to lessen the huge fury which was unfairly misdirected at Wallis he went on to say, somewhat amusingly: "The other person most nearly concerned has tried, up to the last, to persuade me to take a different course." His thoughtful and eloquent speech was edited by none other than the great orator, Winston Churchill.

Edward Albert Christopher George Andrew Patrick David (Windsor)

The Prince of Wales (Right) with his brother Prince Albert "Bertie" aboard

The Renown, world tour 1922

Chapter 3

YOUNG UPSTART

Upon my graduation from Georgetown University in 1970 at the height of the Viet Nam war and student unrest, I married. My new bride, Deloris, and I moved to Ithaca, New York so I could attend graduate school at Cornell University. Deloris' farther, Martin Rosemort was a reformed Mennonite and owner of a firm that designed hospitals in Canada and the US. The Rosemort Design Group had enjoyed a prosperous period during the era when hospitals were built in large numbers throughout the United States. The Hospital Survey and Construction Act (also called the Hill-Burton Act) was President Truman's plan to improve the nation's antiquated hospitals and provide modern facilities allocating "4.5 beds per 1,000 people." The Act was set to expire in 1973 which, not coincidentally, was matched with a rapid decline in hospital construction. This unfortunate business trend overlapped another problem at The Rosemort Design Group: A series of egomaniacal managerial blunders had caused an exodus of the most competent and experienced consultants and architects. This egress spawned several competitors who were soaking up an ever-larger part of a rapidly shrinking market.

Martin and his wife, Miriam, had "come out" of their different but equally restrictive and impoverished childhoods in a big way. Their brief success had gone to their heads and while mirroring what the French call "taking your desires for realities," lived an extravagant life which they increasingly could ill afford. Martin had progressed from a childhood of no entertainment, dancing, or enjoyment to a life of lavishness with tailor made suits and luxurious automobiles. The humorless Miriam was not at all amused when I once told her a joke, "Why can't Mennonites make love standing up? Because God may think they were dancing."

Martin's early years were mainly composed of reading the Bible in rural Manitoba, Canada. Yet, as an adult, he bought an honorary doctorate from George Washington University for $500,000 and sent his family, in first class cabins aboard luxury liners, to Europe each summer. The agoraphobic Miriam was a heavy drinker and chronic smoker. She did not fly or socialize and had converted Martin to Episcopalian. They raised two daughters. Deloris, the oldest, was in my class at Georgetown University and we dated for the last two years of college.

Deloris fought constantly and bitterly with Martin about the war and the student protests at their formal dinners, amusingly served by a British butler. The poor fellow carried oversized silver platters with well cooked meals and was obliged to behave as if in a large British manor house when, in reality, the Rosemort's lived in an unassuming rambler outside of Washington, DC. Perpetuating the silly ruse, the women "retired to the drawing room" after dinner while "the men" drank Port at the dining room table. These were welcome breaks from the heated arguments between Deloris and Martin.

It was in such a forum that Martin gradually began to lament about the increasing number of "defections" from his firm and the growing cash flow crisis. As I approached graduation from college at Georgetown University, I agreed to get an MBA in hospital administration from a respected program and, after that, enter the firm – assuming it still existed.

In 1972, I graduated from Cornell. Meanwhile, due to a lack of new hospital design contracts, the Rosemort Design Group was barely a going concern. The remaining consultants and architects were all on the lookout for more secure positions and we were scurrying to identify new work. I read every "RFP" (request for proposal) from the various government departments relating to hospital design, construction or renovation projects. The days when we had enjoyed working for the Department of Defense and the Veterans Administration were also gone as those projects were being awarded to a number of more reliable competitors as a result of poor Rosemort follow through.

In early 1973, I read an RFP from USAID, a part of the State Department, to rebuild the famous International Hospital of Paris. Having grown up in Europe, the son of a Frenchman, I had known from my earliest recollections about the prominent health care facility. For several decades, anyone who could afford it made certain that they traveled to the International Hospital of Paris for diagnosis and treatments.

The hospital had begun in 1910 with only twenty-four beds intended to offer care for visiting foreigners, notably Americans. Later, the hospital was rebuilt and relocated on the Avenue Charles DeGaulle in Paris' upscale suburb of Neuilly-sur-Seine. By 1970, this second hospital was an aging, patched up facility that needed renovation to maintain its standing. An act of Congress in 1918 gave the International Hospital of Paris a unique status as an institution owned by the American people, allowed to practice medicine in France. It was tasked to serve both French and foreigners, but it was never "conventionné" (reimbursed by the French national health insurance) and, consequently, became a hospital which primarily catered to the rich and famous. Patients came from the world over in search of the highest level of medical care delivered, in part, by a small number of American physicians who were exempt from attending French medical schools or even conforming to French medical accreditations.

In the early 1970's, the hospital was still being heavily subsidized by the US Congress and enjoyed relatively small "line item" grants which were obscure bits and pieces at the bottom of huge bills that Otto Passman's powerful committee approved. The hospital was accredited by what was then called the JCHA (Joint Commission of Hospital Accreditation) which meant that patient care must be delivered in accordance with "proper American standards." The lax performance requirements coupled with the growing lack of medical diligence was a prescription for both medical arrogance and serious legal problems.

Physical plant renovation was not the only long overdue need. The hospital and its physicians had been allowed to simply rest on their laurels. The physical plant had not been upgraded since the end of World War II and the physicians had become accustomed to charging outrageous fees often solely determined on a wealthy patient's ability to pay. Attending ongoing medical education programs or even allowing medical students to observe the level of medicine being practiced was certainly not on the schedules of the senior medical staff members. The famous institution was literally on the verge of physical, administrative and medical collapse and scandal. Its famous Board of Governors was sitting on a ticking time bomb.

USAID's division called American Schools and Hospitals Abroad (ASHA) currently controls 198 institutions in 62 countries; two in

France: The American Library of Paris and the International Hospital of Paris. Before it modernized and expanded its mission to address current international issues, USAID was a remnant of an era past and included The International Hospital of Paris, The American Hospital of Poland and the American University of Beirut. Of all the institutions, it was the International Hospital of Paris which was both the most famous and the most in need of immediate attention. Consequently, the "request for proposal" was issued by USAID to solicit bids to study both the hospital's antiquated management and to prepare a proposal for both organizational changes and, hopefully, physical plant replacement. Among other requirements for a firm, or group of companies, desirous of bidding for the large and prestigious contract was a recent French speaking graduate of an American MBA program with a major in hospital administration.

"Martin," I said to my father-in-law, I think we need to bid on this RFP for the International Hospital of Paris. It may be tailor made for us."

"France is a developing country. I will never forget that you allowed bidets instead of showers in that hospital in Lyon," he exclaimed.

There were several, huge gaps in Martin's progression from Mennonite boy to sophisticate. While attending Cornell University and due to family connections, I was lucky to be hired as a design consultant for a new private hospital in Lyon, France. That particular hospital was to be "conventionné" which meant that we had to adapt our design to French regulations in order to maximize government reimbursement. The famous French pharmaceutical magnet, Doctor Charles Mérieux, had insisted that we be hired. I was extremely flattered by the vote of confidence as well as his ongoing support. Soon he would also be instrumental at the International Hospital in Paris.

"No, Martin," I responded, "France happens to be a permanent member of the United Nation's Security Council but that's not the point. The International Hospital of Paris is exactly that, an American hospital which operates in Paris. They are not subject to French legislation like we were in Lyon."

"I will only work there if they accept my advanced design concepts," he continued with a refrain I had often had to endure.

"Actually, Martin, the RFP is more focused on a management study with a possible, subsequent redesign of the facility. Because of a few odd coincidences, I think we may be able to bid for, and maybe win, the contract. They want a recent graduate of a hospital administration program who is fluent in French. We have not had a new project in six months," I continued.

"Will they forego bidets?" he persisted.

"I have no idea Martin," I responded exasperated, "we are not even in discussions and far from the design phase. The RFP calls for a management review first," I repeated.

"Do whatever you like," he concluded, "but there will never be a bidet in a Rosemort hospital again!"

I worked nonstop, eighteen hour days responding to the RFP which seemed out of our crippled company's reach. We even purchased a new, modern typewriter which was an early version of a word processor to complete the document in the most professional format available. The period between submission and a response seemed interminable. And then, one day, my secretary sported a broad smile upon my return from lunch.

"What would you like more than anything else?" she asked.

"No more calls from bill collectors," I answered.

"Would you accept an invitation to speak with Arturo Costantino?" she said laughing.

Arturo Costantino was the head of American Schools and Hospitals Abroad located at the State Department, only blocks away from our offices on "M" Street in Washington, DC from which we were being evicted for past due rent.

My heart beat so hard I feared it would fly out of my mouth when I first went to Costantino's large office in the impressive State Department building. Although many years separated us, we had an immediate rapport.

"Mr. Silvin, I have read your proposal to provide services at the International Hospital of Paris," he began shocking me by calling me "Mr." "What I like is your education and recent experience in Lyon. What bothers me, however, is your age and the ability of the Rosemort Group to carry though on a high-profile project that will last several years as well as the company's typical; focus on hospital design not management."

"I can't hide my age, sir, but I can assure you that we have a management consultant on staff who is a former senior consultant at Booze Allen Hamilton." Bob Drake was indeed a seasoned management consultant with experience in the emerging specialty of hospital management but who had left the famous consulting firm due to a severe drinking problem.

"Interesting," continued Costantino. "I'd like to see you have a crack at this project but the decision will be made by the Board of Governors of the hospital. If I were you, I'd try to join forces with a large architectural firm interested in the project. You could bring them a needed – and missing – ingredient of French capability and hospital experience and they can bring you credibility."

"We have worked for S.O.M. Have they responded to the RFP?"

S.O.M. stood for the eminent Skidmore Owings and Merrill which had hundreds of architects and had completed several major hospital projects. The previous year I had worked with the Chicago office on a study for the Algerian government to build two University Hospitals in Algeria. The legendary residential architect, Frank Lloyd Wright had amusingly renamed S.O.M as Skiddings, Own-more and Peril.

"Every major American architectural firm has responded," said Costantino. "There will be a fierce fight to land the most prestigious hospital project in the world. It would not be appropriate for me to tell you which consortiums are bidding and which firms are being favored." After a deliberate pause, the man who was obviously trying to mentor me, continued cautiously: "I think I would approach a national firm which has high visibility and recent experience in Washington," he concluded with words that registered immediately.

When I returned to the Rosemort office I wondered if I could fend off our impending eviction. I immediately went to Bob Drake's office. When I related my recent conversation Bob said, "That's clear to me. They like John Carl Warnecke."

The name was indeed famous and very visible in Washington DC. The controversial new library at Georgetown University, which opened during my senior year, had been designed by his firm. It was known that John Warnecke was a personal friend of President Kennedy's and the family had selected him to design the slain President's permanent grave site. Warnecke had also recently completed a spectacular, large renovation of all the buildings along Lafayette Square across from the White House.

On a speaker phone, Bob and I reached Mr. Warnecke who agreed to meet us at his Fifth Avenue office in New York the following day. The firm was finalizing a presentation to the President of the International Hospital's Board of Governors, Perry Culley. He said that it was "possible" to include us in that program if we emphasized our experience in dealing with French legislation and hospital management.

The Warnecke office was dramatic and impressive. The 1970's also happened to represent the cresting of *their* reputation. It would have been impossible to imagine that the prestigious firm would have to be sold fifteen years later to avoid bankruptcy and Mr. Warnecke would struggle to keep his New York home and his prized vineyard in Sonoma, California.

When I met him and his senior executives, however, they were aglow with the completion of the State Capital Building in Hawaii and had 125 architects plus support staff housed in four offices throughout the United States. While not as large as S.O.M., it certainly was as respectable and well connected politically. Mr. Warnecke was personable and inquisitive; he agreed to include me in their presentation to the International Hospital's board chairman the following week at their office, followed by drinks in an "intimate setting" at his Park Avenue apartment.

Had I realized how important that meeting was to me and my in-law's future, I would have been much more nervous. To add to the possible tension was the fact that Bob Drake had begun drinking again. Oblivious to the issues surrounding me, I was enthused with a "high tech" slide show I put together detailing the Lyon project which I had also been allowed to use for my comprehensive exams at Business School. It included specifics of differences between American and French medicine and hospital management and design.

The first time I saw Perry Culley at the Warnecke office, I was immediately impressed with his presence and how he commanded the attention of everyone in a room. He had the ability to put me, and the architects making the presentation with me, at ease in spite of the importance of the meeting. I hoped Perry and I would be friends for life but could not have dreamed that, fifteen years later, I would be given the honor to be his daughter's God-father. Perry Culley was the finest example of a refined career public servant, unhappily married to the perfect career diplomat's wife. After serving as an intelligence officer during the Second World War, he had filled many important diplomatic missions around the world. He was a Francophile who was a knowledgeable connoisseur and lover of French culture. His current ambassadorial position was as Deputy Chief of Mission of the American Embassy in Paris, typically the number two position in an embassy. He smoked constantly during the two and a half hour session which included forty-five minutes of my presentation and concluded with saying "very interesting" in an enthusiastic manner and repeating "very interesting."

Within a week, in mid June, we made an instant replay in France of the now well tailored presentation to the selection committee of

The International Hospital's Governors who rapidly made the final decision to hire the Warnecke-Rosemort team which also included the well-known engineering firm of Syska and Hennessey. A month later, in late July, 1973, Deloris and I moved to France with Bob Drake and Chris von Steibuchel, a young German architect, who served as a space planner on Rosemort's dwindling staff. Von Steinbuchel's father owned a respected architectural firm in Frankfurt, Germany and, as such, Chris was not vulnerable to working with people on the verge of bankruptcy.

The projected detailed expenses of my small site office in Paris represented only 10% of Rosemort's total operating budget while the revenues represented 60% of their needs. Needless to say there was great excitement that the Rosemort name had the potential to be continued and the exodus of staff might be halted. To express his elation, Martin bought Miriam a sable coat and sent us off, in first class, aboard the Italian Line's flagship, Michelangelo, with my sports car and our dog, Robbie.

Robbie was not the only dog in the ship's kennel moving to Europe on that nine day crossing from New York to Cannes, France. While walking Robbie on deck, and sneaking him to our cabin, we befriended a young, mysterious, bearded American traveling with his English sheep dog. He introduced himself as "Paco" and clearly was not interested in any small talk or professional discussion. He was the only attendee in the first class dining room that refused to wear a tuxedo, ate alone and wore a blue jean jacket and neck beads. Only on our arrival in Europe, did he admit that he was "Serpico," the honest cop who had been shot in the head while he was attempting to expose corruption in the NYPD. The story later became a successful film starring Al Pacino.

In the last scene of the movie, the viewer sees Serpico, sitting with his dog, on a New York City pier waiting to board a transatlantic liner. Frank Serpico had completed his consulting work on the soon-to-be released movie. He was fleeing the New York police force to immigrate to Villars, Switzerland, a place where I had spent three years in my early childhood at a Swiss boarding school.

Deloris was thrilled to be leaving her father, Martin, and their arguments. She was overly eager to assume a position in a social setting in Paris and we were both ecstatic about what we naively thought was a solution to the chronic and debilitating Rosemort financial problems.

Chapter 4

NEUILLY-SUR-SEINE

On a flash trip to Paris, before we moved, I rented a pleasant, yet unassuming apartment on the top floor of a relatively new apartment building on the Rue de Longchamps – not far from the hospital. Over the decades, The International Hospital had acquired numerous adjacent villas and other buildings and owned almost the entire square, city block. Only a few neighbors had resisted the various approaches to sell their properties. One small villa on the site was allocated to us where we set up a sparse but comfortable conference room in what had been the villa's living room. Chris, the young architect, installed drawing boards in the previous dining room for himself and two draftsmen we hoped to hire. The plan was for Chris to prepare schematic, to scale drawings of a phased total reconstruction of the hospital. The scheme had to be conceived in such a way as to keep the facility fully operational during the three year construction period. Once we had completed that part of the contract, the Warnecke architects would convert our "single line drawings" into the "working drawings" that the eventual contractor would use to build the new hospital.

Of immediate concern to USAID was the preparation of a management assessment. So, on the first floor of the villa, we used the wide hallway for two secretaries and then designated the two large bedrooms for my and Bob's offices where we would run a temporary administration of the facility. The two smaller bedrooms would be used for associate hospital administrators.

Before I could begin work, however, I had to obtain both a French Government work permit and a residence permit. I had been assigned an officer at the Unites States Embassy located on a corner of the magnificent Place de la Concorde, in central Paris, to facilitate the few bureaucratic hurdles we had to cross. Every time I was on the famous sixteen acre "square," I was acutely aware of its fascinating history. It was created by King Louis XV in 1772 and named after him as long as his statue stood in the middle of the square. Twenty years later, after the French revolution it appropriately became the "Place de la Révolution" (Revolution Square) and a Guillotine occupied the spot where the King's figure had proudly stood. During the ensuing two years, over one thousand beheadings were carried out there including King Louis XVI and his wife, Marie-Antoinette. Finally, in 1830, the 100 foot, three thousand year old, pink marble obelisk from the Egyptian King, Ramses II's temple, replaced the Guillotine and is there to this day.

Two immaculately uniformed marines stood at attention at the front door of the embassy whenever I went in to see David Katz, my liaison officer.

"I have arranged for you to have private meetings with both the city and the Ministry of Labor to facilitate the issuance of the permits you need to be legal," he said amicably. "What can be a horrendous process should be easy given the level of people you will meet and the fact that you are under contract with The Department of State."

My first meeting was with a deputy assistant minister of labor who greeted me with a broad smile when I entered his office a few days after we arrived in Paris. I quickly learned that the smile was sarcastic because, after he ushered me over to a conference table which bore my open file, he went directly to the point.

"You do not need a work permit in France, Mr. Silvin" he said to my surprise.

"Very well, thank you Monsieur. I was ill advised by the embassy and will go straight to work at the hospital."

"No," he continued "you do not understand. Katz was correct in setting up this appointment but what he did not know is that you are French and, as such, you do not require a work permit."

"My father was French," I responded. "I only have an American passport."

"That is not relevant to us," he tried to clarify. "Once French, always French and while you may not consider yourself as a citizen of France, we do."

"Well, I suppose I have wasted enough of your time," I said standing and becoming a bit uncomfortable with the direction of the conversation. "Forgive me."

"You still do not understand," he persisted. "You cannot work at the International Hospital. You will have to serve for two years in one of France's armed forces. You have to present yourself to one of these addresses at once to enlist," he concluded smiling.

"You are joking, right?" I inquired.

"Not at all Monsieur, I am afraid you cannot work here without first completing the required military service."

I raced back to the embassy and, when I told David Katz what I had learned, he brought me to meet Arthur "Dick" Watson, the outgoing American ambassador. Watson was the son of Thomas John Watson Sr. the founder of IBM and the brother of Thomas Watson Jr. who succeeded his late father at the head of the rapidly growing computer giant. He had been assigned to Paris as a consolation prize because he was never going to ascend to the executive offices at the giant company his father had created. The problem was his heavy and constant drinking which would also be the cause for his brief eighteen month tenure as Ambassador to France during which he had attracted many other IBM associates to Paris.

The Ambassador's nickname was ironic indeed. Like his brother and father, the Watson men were good looking. "Dick" was also a roué and a rogue. He relished in unusual sexual conquest which, given his name and stature, were the subject of many jokes and rumors. One such story was that Dick slept with three generations of women from the same, well known Parisian family: grandmother, mother and daughter. Each had received expensive jewelry bought at Van Cleef and Arpel near the Ritz Hotel on Place Vendome.

When I arrived in France, Watson was being replaced by his brother-in-law, John N. Irwin, who was married to Jeanette Watson. The prestigious, highly visible and social position of American Ambassador to France would remain in the Watson family. Irwin's tenure as Ambassador would happen to coincide with mine at the hospital. Amusingly when Watson flew back to the US, he became so intoxicated in the upstairs lounge of a TWA 747 he fought with other passengers who wanted to use the space which was available to all first class passengers. He rose angrily, fell down the spiral stairs and broke his collarbone. Less than two years later, in July, 1974 Watson died in his home in New Canaan, Connecticut. He was 55 years old.

While Ambassador Watson listened to my predicament, he was clearly distracted by the preparations for his imminent departure and I certainly was the least of his concerns. He did say that he would "bring the matter up with the Secretary of State's office" and assumed it would be "handled." I was too young and naïve to imagine that he could be correct.

Amazingly it *was* "handled" and I was quickly issued a foreigner's work permit without ever returning the Ministry of Labor. The document allowed me to work at both the International Hospital and any other hospital in France and would have to be reviewed every two years. When David Katz handed me the document he added "I think you can skip going to the Town Hall in Neuilly for a living permit. You will never have any problems." But David was wrong.

Bob and I spent our first months with each department head, interviewed all the physicians and Board members as well as hospital staff at all levels. One problem we had was that most of the staff had signed up with the CGT, the French Communist Party workers union. Prior managerial miscalculations at the hospital had created a hostile and adversarial situation which led to the communist union being represented in the hospital.

We were obliged to open our offices and files to their employee representative who searched through our notes with neurotic suspicion and followed up by demanding many explanations. Consequently, Bob and I had to have private discussions away from the hospital and our offices. These conversations, at my apartment, centered on how shocked we were with the lack of any proper management techniques. We began writing the report that would eventually be presented to the Board of Governors and in order to keep Bob sober, I pretended that my bar was empty.

From our offices we also handled the Rosemort Group's other active European contract which was as design consultant to the City of Cologne for the replacement of the vast 2,200 bed University Hospital. Chris and I traveled to Cologne every week for two days of meetings carrying tubes of rolled architectural drawings and briefcases full of files. Our contract with USAID allowed for specific absences for each of us from the International Hospital to pursue other activities so I also spent a day each week trying to market our services to other hospitals in need of planning new facilities.

The marketing efforts quickly produced another hospital design project in Paris. A handsome and debonair young physician had recently married the only daughter of Homer Deberry, her family was prepared to fund the construction of a private hospital from which he would become well known and successful in his own right. The proposed high end clinic would also be built in exclusive Neuilly.

Homer Deberry was a famous, even infamous, French politician who, over his long career had become a somewhat feared household word. In his youth, he was a lawyer in his native Corsica and then became active in the French resistance during the Second World War. He was the head of Charles de Gaulle's brutal personal security force when the General was in Algeria as well as when de Gaulle returned to a liberated Paris in 1944. Deberry held the dual positions of Mayor of Neuilly and Congressman (Député) for several decades of autocratic rule in Neuilly. In 1969, and until my arrival in France, he also filled the important role of President of the "Assemblée Nationale," France's equivalent of our House of Representatives. As is the case with the American Speaker of the House, he was third in line to the French Presidency. His male secretary had a young son, Nicolas Sarkozy, who Deberry mentored and who is currently the new French President. Eventually it would be Deberry, as Mayor of Neuilly, who would have to approve the building plan for the International Hospital, a critical step which concerned both John Warnecke and USAID.

Shortly after I met Dominique, Deberry's petite and sexy daughter, and her charming physician husband, Michel, Deloris and I began spending fun-filled weekends at luxury hotels in various parts of rural France. We were all interested in French history and, surprisingly, our new friends had not visited the famous historic castles of the Loire Valley. We decided to make a carefully planned tour of many of them together. Every time we registered at a hotel, it was obvious that the staff was impressed and even in awe that Homer Deberry's daughter was in the hotel for the weekend with her husband, their body-guard and her young American friends. Obviously, we never encountered bad service or food whether in Normandy, Britany, Auvergne or Provence. During walks and horseback rides in the woods, glider flying lessons and long, gourmet French dinners Michel asked many details about hospital design and management. Eventually, we brought him to meet the owners of the hospital that the Rosemort Group had designed in Lyon. I had become good friends with the pro-prietor physician shareholders and they were pleased to open their books to us. The result was that Dominique and Michel convinced her father to back a proposed hospital that we would design, and per-haps manage and that Deberry would own. Michel would be Chief of Staff and a publicist would transform him into a famous French surgeon.

While exciting in its early stages, the relationship would soon become filled with complicated intrigue and present a huge challenge for both me and the International Hospital.

Chapter 5

INSIDE THE INTERNATIONAL
HOSPITAL OF PARIS

Two separate sets of meetings were scheduled with the senior members of the medical staff and department heads. One group of interviews would be conducted by Bob and me to create a management assessment and report. The second series of interviews would be held with Chris to document physical plant limitations and the requirements for the new hospital.

There were six permanent American physicians on staff and some two dozen French doctors and surgeons who had very valuable and lucrative admitting privileges. The vast majority of our interviews were non-confrontational and informative. However, two important physicians were instantly suspicious of our arrival at the hospital and fearful of any changes we might recommend which could ultimately result in a reduction of their authority and, consequently, income.

Sheldon Cheek was the Chief of Staff who had held the all-powerful position for many years during which no one had challenged his medical, ethical of financial decisions. He was a short, thin, balding man with clammy hands and a suspicious look.

"We notice with some concern," I began after the requisite small talk "that the hospital has no infection committee."

All reputable American hospitals monitor the infection rates with a committee which reports to the Chief of Staff and the concerned department heads on how the infection rates compare to prior periods as well as regional and national rates of infections. Without such a report there is no way to monitor any increase of infections, the occurrence of new types of infections and which areas in the facility (and which physicians) may be responsible for spreading them.

"We don't need an infection committee, gentleman," he responded with an arrogant tone we would come to know all too well. "The International Hospital is the finest hospital in Europe. Everyone knows that. Why alarm people with sneaky committees?"

"Doctor," said Bob, "if we are to obtain an American accreditation, it is imperative that we document infections. We have no intention of sneaking around. Also, I am sorry to say that from our unofficial observations and review of medical records, infections appear to be rampant."

"That's a bunch of crap," responded the Chief of Staff.

"The next issue of some concern," I said changing the subject but not for the better, "is the absence of a tissue committee."

Such a commission would monitor what percentage of healthy versus infected or necrotic tissue was removed in surgery. Without this information, no administrator could evaluate which surgeons were perfuming necessary operations instead of frivolous, unnecessary ones.

"You'll have to take that up with the chief of surgery, Professor Chevalier," said Cheek. "And I'd recommend you inform yourselves about his reputation before you assault him about an infection committee."

"I am well aware of the Professor's reputation," I said trying to hide any hint of sarcasm. "We have found that surgeons with low infection rates are proud of the fact and like to have these reports prepared and circulated." Our review of surgery patients' charts had revealed what would be an alarming infection rate in any hospital.

"Circulated?" yelled Cheek.

"Yes, doctor, the best physicians want such information to be available to their patents as well as the hospital's administration" I said.

"Ridiculous!" spat Cheek. "You guys better be very careful."

"Just one more thing, doctor," I said. "Has the use of identification bracelets on the patients never been suggested?"

"Can you imagine asking Madame de Rothschild to remove her diamonds and replace them with plastic?" he asked contemptuously. Cheek boasted all over Paris that he was the personal physician of the de Rothschild family.

"Well, Doctor, I assume Madame de Rothschild leaves her diamonds at home when she is hospitalized and that she would appreciate some assurance that she will be given the proper medication if she is asleep when a nurse enters her room with a syringe."

"You guys are going to have a very rough time here if you try to run this place as if it were an American hospital," said Cheek.

"But, Doctor, it is an American hospital and must be run in accordance with commonly accepted American medical procedures and practices," said Bob.

"We'll see about that. Perhaps you forgot that I recently became a full member of the Board of Governors. I wonder what they will think about this?" mumbled the Chief of Staff ending the meeting.

After leaving Cheek's office, Bob inquired, "Did they teach you at Cornell why it is ill advised to have physicians serve on a hospital's Board?"

"No," I answered, "but it's clear as to why they should not."

"The problem we are going to have here," explained Bob, "is that the Board is overly involved in the day to day running of the hospital. To make things worse the only medical advice they will get is from that clown. You must understand that, if our report is to be truthful and of value, it will step on a lot of toes. This could get very rough."

"Well we'll fasten our seatbelts," I said quoting Betty Davis' famous line in *All About Eve*.

Bob, Chris and my meeting with the famed Professor Chevalier would be no more reassuring or sensible. We met him as a trio because we would be discussing both design and managerial issues. As Chief of Surgery, Doctor Chevalier controlled which French physicians could operate in "his" surgical suite and, using an antiquated system, he charged other surgeons a fee to be allowed to operate using his name. In addition to rampant infections in the OR, we had been well informed of the "taxation" Chevalier and some other department heads were practicing.

While we tried to establish some sense of ease with the rotund, square and red faced Chevalier, he abruptly said:

"I insist that the new hospitals' operating suite be located on the top floor of the new building."

"Professor," I answered, "that type of design has been surpassed. Modern hospitals have a diagnostic and treatment center that is adjacent to the bed tower, not atop it. In that way we can use less expensive materials to build it and have a more flexible structural system that has larger spans between the vertical supports. We can create better working spaces, well adapted to their purpose rather than being restricted to a structural system required to support a bed tower. This also maximizes the ability to have future expansions of certain departments."

"I don't care about that at all," he explained. "I need to see the Eiffel Tower when I operate. It inspires me. And flies cannot reach the top floor of the hospital."

Chris, Bob and I looked at each other in disbelief. Finally, Chris tried again:

"Professor, modern operating rooms have no windows. There is a triple corridor plan used to separate clean and soiled traffic patterns to reduce infection. The operating rooms are surrounded by corridors."

"I need open windows in my OR," he persisted.

"Again, Professor," Chris interjected, "there will be no windows in the diagnostic and treatment center. It will be completely air conditioned and climate controlled. I assure you there will be no flies, Professor."

"Another thing, gentleman," continued Chevalier, "I insist on having my surgical tools sterilized in the OR."

"Again, Doctor," Bob interjected a bit exasperated, "modern hospitals worldwide centralize all decontamination and sterilization functions in a single area. That way we can have the best double door washer-sterilizers for all soiled supplies and equipment. The days when each department - such as surgery, obstetrics and pathology – had their own equipment to wash and sterilize are over."

"You do not understand," said Chevalier. "I like to bring my own operating utensils *to* the operating room."

Again, my team and I looked at each other in disbelief as we began to understand why the International Hospital's infection rates were off the charts.

"Doctor," I said, "you will be able to special order any utensils you like but they will not leave the hospital and they will be sterilized centrally. We will prepare surgical packs for each surgeon, specially assembled by procedure."

"No, I reject that," he answered. "If I am to be held responsible for the sterility of my instruments, they will be washed under my direction."

"Is that an efficient use of your talents?" I asked hoping to lighten the moment.

"Do you have sterilizers which are routinely checked for accuracy and which shut off if the temperature drops below 180 degrees?" asked Chris, knowing the antiquated equipment the hospital owned and fearing what primitive techniques Chevalier may have at home.

Thus the tone of our relationship with Chevalier was established. It was impossible to obtain any information on the space requirements or, importantly, if young surgeons might be recruited to expand and update the hospital's surgical specialties and capabilities.

Bob and I proceeded to secretively assemble the material for our report, Chris began his drawings for the replacement hospital without the input of irrational physicians and I implemented several managerial changes. These included both a tissue and an infection committee.

It was the violent reaction by Doctor Cheek and Professor Chevalier to these committees that gave me the title of "young upstart" and created the need to have the matter brought up to the full Board of Governors including Chairman Passman and the Duchess of Windsor. Fortunately for me, Wallis was determined to see me vindicated regardless of her deteriorating health.

Part Two

POLITICS

Chapter 1

THE BOARD OF GOVERNORS

In 1973, there were a grand total of twenty-four members of the International Hospital's Board of Governors. The American Ambassador to France served as "Honorary President" of the Board, while the General Council of the US Embassy was "Honorary Vice-President." Unlike some of the other honorary members, the Ambassador and General Council never attended meetings. However, the two honorary members who frequently did participate were The Duchess of Windsor and General Robert A. Solberg.

The General was in his early nineties when we met. I was enthralled with his unusual past and he was happy to speak with a curious, young man desirous to learn about his fascinating long life. Having been born in Tsarist Russia in the early 1880's, General Solberg served in Tsar Nicholas' army as a young lieutenant, fighting against Germany in World War I, before the Russian Revolution. The General was generous in his vivid descriptions of an era which he had experienced and is now gone forever. I was delighted to listen. General Solberg also held the position of Chairman of the hospital's "Building and Equipment Committee"; this gave us a business reason to work together.

Robert Solberg was one of a few dedicated soldiers to serve as an officer of both the Russian and American military. Before the Russian Revolution, and dating back to the American War of Independence when Catherine the Great sent soldiers to fight on the American' behalf, the Russian and American armies were strong, collaborating allies. After his naturalization, Solberg became a senior officer in the American army, ultimately rising to the rank of General after the Second World War. Given his experiences, he certainly was not impressed or intimidated by the antics of the senior members of The International Hospital's medical staff. Nor was he shy in expressing any of his concerns. As a result, he was one of my few early supporters. He was visibly relieved when my team and I showed up in Paris. Our presence gave him the ability to counter certain physician requests for unnecessary or inappropriate equipment with facts. On one occasion, upon entering the Boardroom, he looked first at Doctor Cheek and then at me and said in a loud voice, "It's good to see you here my young friend. Perhaps you can add some sanity to these meetings."

Any business school teaches its students that the efficacy of a board lessens as the number of members exceeds twelve to fifteen. The fact that many of twenty-four members of the International Hospital's Board did not regularly attend meetings did not improve the situation. There were an additional twenty "Honorary Members" included in the Board's total tally. This situation typically created a delay as members who were usually in attendance had to spend time briefing those who had not been present. Furthermore, what was conspicuously missing was the presence of respected French names. Even though we were "an American hospital," all hospitals need to be represented by well informed and influential locals. Shortly after I arrived in Paris, I recommended to the Board's President, Perry Culley, that we establish a "French Advisory Committee" to fill the void.

At exactly ten o'clock on the day of the Board meeting which I so feared, the members and guests started to move over in the direction of the large boardroom table where we all took our seats. This was an important meeting which would start on time because both the Duchess and Chairman Passman were attending. I was extremely nervous about what I knew would be an assault by the Chief of Staff, possibly resulting in my dismissal. This would also likely mean terminating the Rosemort contract and could spell bankruptcy for my in-laws. My anxiety had not been much reduced by the Duchess's earlier reassuring words:

"Just stay calm. He is a pompous and arrogant man." I knew that the Duchess had a fight instinct and an ability to adamantly, often sarcastically, prove her point. Nevertheless I *was* very nervous.

Perry Culley, looking dapper as usual and completely in control, called the meeting to order. He sat in the middle of a long table with the Duchess on his right and Chairman Passman was positioned across from him. I sat at the far end of the table while Cheek took a seat at the opposite end. As a result the Chief of Staff and I were as far from each other as possible. After the usual agenda items such as approving the minutes from the previous meeting were covered, the subject of creating a few new outpatient clinics was addressed.

"I see that there is a request to start a VD clinic at the hospital," said Passman laughing.

"I find it incredible that y'all don't already have one."

The Duchess was in a fine mood and ready to engage. "Do you mean to imply, Mr. Chairman, that you have actually had VD?" she asked in a tone of both amusement and sarcasm followed by her hearty laugh.

"Had it, Duchess?" he responded. "Good God, Madam, I was state distributor!"

The Duchess was neither unnerved nor amused by the inappropriate comment. During her notorious past she had heard and, indeed said, numerous things which were more risqué than the chairman's bad joke. Her blank look indicated that the humor might be acceptable after a long dinner among close friends but not in this context. After an uncomfortable silence with all members taking close notice of her demeanor, Perry brought the discussion to the next agenda item.

"Doctor Cheek, our Chief of Staff, has asked to make a presentation. Doctor Cheek, the floor is yours."

Cheek did not rise. He shot a quick look at me and then addressed the group.

"I wish my first presentation could be more positive, but a serious matter is at hand. Several physicians have expressed concern to me about the new administrative practices that the Rosemort consultants have proposed. We feel that there is an assault on our integrity and that Silvin and his team have not taken our, shall I say, special situation into consideration. He wants the International Hospital to function like any community hospital in the United States and that would simply be inappropriate." The doctor paused as the few members who had not been informed of the scheduled showdown leaned forward to learn more.

"No one has ever questioned our medical ability and I, for one, find this attack to be a battering of my reputation," he concluded.

As if at a tennis tournament, all heads turned towards me to respond.

"Duchess," I began by addressing the only lady present besides the secretary who was taking notes, "Mister Chairman, gentlemen, allow me to respond. Under no circumstances have I, or my colleague Bob Drake, made any assault on Doctor Cheek. Could you please clarify and explain, doctor?" I said trying to get him to reveal the real problem.

"Yes," he almost shouted. "This infection and tissue committee business is not only pure folly but it is insulting. And I refuse to put plastic bracelets on my hospitalized patients."

The heads all bobbed back to my end of the table. I gave a brief explanation of how these committees function and what they were meant to monitor. I concluded with my old refrain, "Physicians who do well on these subjects have nothing to worry about. In fact they are always proud to reveal the results. In the US, more and more patients are actually asking physicians for a review of how they score on these matters. Frankly, I would be very concerned if my doctor refused to reveal to me – as his or her patient – what the results are."

"My patients have no interest in grilling me," continued a now red-faced Cheek. "They come to us because of our outstanding reputation. And I will take this one step further. I have discussed this with Genevieve Pray, who is so upset that she is considering removing the hospital from both her annual donation and her will if my integrity continues to be brought into question by a young…."He paused wondering, I suppose how harsh his words should be, "…a young upstart who is not even a physician."

Genevieve Pray was Achille-Fould's sister. The well known banking family had spawned many French Ministers over several centuries and its ancestral home was the elite eighteenth century Chateau de Beychevelle in the Médoc wine producing section of France. This home is one of the best examples of pure Louis XV architectural design. Its original owner served as King Louis XV's finance minister and the chateau had recently passed on to Genevieve and Aymar Achille-Fould, Mrs. Pray's brother, who was serving as Postal Minister of France.

"Doctor Cheek has spoken to us about this also," said Gregory O'Neal, the Rexall Drug and Chemical Company's senior International executive. "My wife was alarmed as well."

"That's interesting," said Charles Torem a preeminent lawyer representing both highly visible personal and corporate American interests from his office as Senior Partner at the prestigious Coudert Brothers law firm. "My wife has also told me of her concern."

The matter was getting grave indeed. I wondered how many more powerful women might have been contacted and how many would actually threaten to remove the hospital from their wills if I were allowed to stay on at my job. But none of those ladies were here and the Duchess' opinion outweighed, indeed could trump, all the others' combined.

"Gentlemen," began the Duchess in her strong yet calm voice, "I find all this very odd indeed. It seems to me that Mr. Silvin is trying to improve the reporting of basic statistics. I have repeatedly said that the International Hospital is one of America's best ambassadors. It would seem to me that we must, therefore, not only follow these modern techniques practiced in the United States but we should encourage them. Are we to lag behind what is being done in America? I am finding it a bit hard to understand. As far as wearing a plastic identification band, I wore them in the United States twenty years ago!" Then leaning forward and looking at me with her piecing, dark blue eyes, she added, "Have you accused Doctor Cheek of any impropriety?"

"No, Duchess," I answered. "If anything, I'd like to give Doctor Cheek and others the ammunition to respond to the rumors in Paris that the International Hospital is antiquated in its medical management and is being surpassed by some private French facilities with younger physicians."

"Well, that sounds rather logical to me," she said looking first at Perry and then across the table toward Chairman Passman. "I rather feel like we need to applaud these efforts." The Duchess was now in full battle mode. She held her head erect showing off her beautiful posture, jutted her prominent chin forward and concluded looking at Cheek, "In fact Doctor, if what you have called the young upstart is *not* allowed to carry forward with what has been described, I'd consider curtailing my donations to the hospital. And I am quite certain that, were he alive, the Duke would concur." She sat perfectly erect, regally cleared her throat, and flashed a quick look at me with her beautiful eyes. After a few uncomfortable seconds of silence, and perhaps believing that she still needed to go further, the Duchess added, "Before I am treated or operated on here again, I will be asking the physician concerned how he or she scores on these tests!" She chuckled to herself.

The reference to her late husband coupled with her great sarcasm about encouraging patients to become better informed when addressing a physician brought the matter to a close. A silence ensued which was broken by the Board's President.

"Shall we move on?" asked Culley.

A series of uncomfortable mumbles followed while the remaining subjects on the agenda were rapidly covered and the bumpy meeting was adjourned. As we all rose to leave the room, the Duchess winked at me and said, "Well then, this matter is over – at least for now. But I want you to meet with Genevieve Pray. She is influential and once she knows you she will never listen to that pompous little man again." Shifting gears she added, "You will accompany me to the gala. Genevieve will be there and I will introduce you. It will be an important evening for us both as it is my first public appearance as a widow. I will send the car to collect you."

The Duchess was referring to a formal dinner party given after the Grand Prix de Paris horse race to benefit the hospital. John Irwin, the new American ambassador would be there and the Duchess had also allowed her name to be used as Honorary Chairwoman for the event. It would be one of the most coveted social occasions for the American community in Paris. On the few occasions the Duchess asked for an escort, one of her cars would first pick him up, and then proceed to Le Bois on the Route du Champ d'Entrainement, the Duchess' home, to collect her. A police car would be waiting to escort them.

Her uniformed butler and a footman met me at the home's oversized colored marble foyer, lit by wall-mounted candelabra. Perry had told me to notice the red box on a table in the entrance marked "The King." It was cleverly placed under a red banner which depicted

Edward's crest – often confused with his grandfather's crest – when he was Prince of Wales. The flag had hung at Windsor castle and the red box was used to carry important documents from Prime Minister Baldwin to Edward when he was King. Waiting patiently, the butler dressed in black tails then brought me into the smaller of the two "drawing rooms" where the Duchess was having a drink. Like her late husband, there were times when she drank a considerable amount. The Duchess liked Champagne or small glasses of vodka. These early days of being alone were one such period of consuming several glasses of vodka before dinner. She sat on a yellow couch near the ox blood fireplace. Above the mantle crowded with beautiful antiques and candelabra, hung atop a huge mirror, was a painting of the Duchess wearing one of her typical, well-tailored, simple yet slightly severe dresses. She beckoned me over to a red Louis XV armchair, ordered the butler to serve me and surprised me by introducing another discussion about ocean liners.

She, like I, loved the great old ships and, naturally, she had much more experience than I. This was not the first time we were discussing her transatlantic adventures. The Duke and she always "crossed" twice a year: once in winter and again in the summer. In the pre and post war years they were loyal to the British Cunard Line with a penchant to travel on the Queen Mary. They always occupied what later became the Winston Churchill suite, located mid-ships on A Deck. Each ritual winter trip they stayed in a magnificent suite which took up the entire twenty-eighth floor at the Waldorf Towers in New York. Their accommodations were immediately above one of their close friends, Elsie Woodward, arguably one of New York's premiere Grande Dames but much less social than Wallis. After the stopover they boarded a train headed to Palm Beach, Florida. They usually traveled to see Robert

Young, the railroad tycoon with whom they often stayed and whose company they had invested in. He always attached his private railway car to their scheduled train in order to bring the Windsor's and their massive collection of luggage to Palm Beach as comfortably as possible.

"I so loved 'The Mary'," said Wallis. "Before we were married, David cut a trip of ours short to stand next to his mother, Queen Mary, when the largest ship in the world was launched in 1935. The Queen dedicated her with David looking on. So, of course, we were partial to her. There really was no equal to The Mary except for The Normandie and David felt that we needed to be loyal to England."

"You did sail on The United States many times, did you not?" I asked.

"Yes," she answered, "The Mary eventually became outdated really when The United States went into service." The Duchess always used the affectionate nickname of "The Mary" for the Queen Mary. She omitted to say that the Cunard line had tired of handling the couple's one hundred pieces of monogrammed Louis Vuitton luggage and ceased housing them in the best suite without charge. When The SS United States began her career in the early 1950's the Royal couple switched their loyalty to the new, modern American ship due to its speed, superior air conditioning and the company's willingness to allow the Duchess to keep her pug dogs in the suite with them rather than in the ship's kennel. Importantly, the line also gave them free passage.

As Raymond Kane, a steward aboard the United States wrote: "The United States line was very, very proud to have the former King of England as a regular passenger. There were no rules for them. It was a priceless testimonial to the company and to the United States. They were the ultimate celebrity passengers back then."

Despite the change in lines, Cunard published a book entitled *Stars Aboard* that stated, "The Windsor's set the seal on a Cunard crossing as the ultimate in chic."

"I suppose the food may have been slightly better on the French line but one shouldn't overeat at sea," she proclaimed. "The only exercise we got was walking around promenade deck after meals. David always wanted to use the outdoor promenade whenever possible and we'd bundle up," she said with a giggle. "And we'd have to look our best as everyone wanted to catch a glimpse of us. We always strolled arm in arm," she said with a sad sigh indicating how much she missed the Duke. "Those were wonderful times," she said and gazed off at his portrait.

"We loved those walks except for the few strangers who insisted on trying to talk to us. It is even said that Cunard's bookings increased to full capacity when the press announced the crossing we were to take."

Each Royal boarding and disembarkation was a major news event in either New York or Cherbourg, France with camera ready reporters eager to take what would be a front page picture. Frequently, the Duke would hold a brief news conference to give superficial details about their travel plans while the Duchess stood nearby holding their dogs.

"Some of those intruders were so tiresome!" she continued and shrugged her shoulders as if to add "so what."

"Luckily we generally traveled with friends and, when necessary, a body-guard who protected us from any abuse." During certain periods both before and after her marriage, the Duchess received death threats which, understandably, frightened her. In addition to friends, they traveled with personal maids and a butler.

The couple had never taken any Italian ships like the Andrea Doria in the 1950's, the beautiful, new Michelangelo or her sister ship, the Raffaello, the following decade. The Italian Line used a longer, more southern route; they boarded passengers in Cannes, first crossed the Mediterranean and then went through the Straits of Gibraltar before making the transatlantic crossing. I had traveled several times on these modern ships. The Duchess was happy to listen to me describe the outdoor living on the famed "Lido Deck" which was designed to take advantage of the warmer, calmer routes. She asked questions about the rakish contemporary design and wondered if the two ships had what she called "adequate suites."

"They seem so very modern," she said with her slight characteristic frown. "I wonder if it will be anything like what we knew… But then again, nothing is the same anymore and I dislike planes so." She then returned to her desire to understand what the best accommodations were like.

"Tell me, do they have dining rooms in their best suites?"

"I crossed once with BoBo Rockefeller who had the best suite on Upper Deck…."

"Never actually met her," interrupted the Duchess. "One hears many stories of course. But they hear many ridiculous stories about me as well!" She laughed bawdily again.

"I like her very much. In some ways you are similar in that you are both nonconformists."

"Nonconformists," she repeated. "That's a good one! I'll take non-conformist over what I am usually called."

"Anyway, Duchess," I continued picking up the lost thread of the conversation. "Bobo had no dining room on the Michelangelo. A lovely sitting room but it was furnished contemporarily. The 'Mike' or the 'Raff' as they are affectionately called are no Queen Mary."

The Italian Line catered to a somewhat younger crowd and presented opportunities to experience a ship-board life very different from what The Windsor's enjoyed as a couple. In their heyday, the Duke and Duchess took some of their meals in their private dining room, or in the small Verandah Grill overlooking the stern of ship which offered spectacular views of the great vessel's wake. The beautiful, wood paneled room is now called The Winston Churchill dining room in the Queen Mary Hotel in Long Beach, California. It boasts several pictures of the Duke and Duchess on the walls while they traveled aboard Cunard's ships. The famous couple only ate in the "regular" first class dining room when they joined the captain at his table. Every eye in the room peered at them, especially at Wallis, to observe every detail: what she wore and which pieces of famous jewelry she had selected for the evening.

I explained that, on the Italian Line, the weather allowed for outdoor dining and late night dancing by the pool located near the ship's great twin, lattice caged funnels. The stacks were beautifully illuminated and first class passengers enjoyed midnight pasta and champagne overlooking them. I would like to think that the description led to the Duchess' first crossing on the Italian Line and that she was able to derive some pleasure on the trip in spite of her remark, "Dancing

outside at midnight? I think those days are well past us now, René."
Wallis occasionally used a royal 'we.' "But we used to love to dance into
the middle of the night years ago. Oh, what fun we had!" She paused
and stared off into the distance.

"Well then," she continued, "I shall try them next year when I make
my first trip back to the States since the Duke passed away. I am a bit
concerned about going to New York so the crossing will give me time
to reflect."

In his memoir, Rosalbo Lottero, a veteran entertainer on the Italian
ships wrote, "Toward the end (of the Italian line), we had the widowed
Duchess of Windsor. She came to dinner each evening, but sometimes
she was confused. She was very old and very frail."

In fact, she was only seventy-nine and partly senile.

I thought of the fascinating love story and, ultimately, "the wedding
of the century" that she and the Duke enjoyed. While the romance
was complicated, convoluted and not free of stress it captured the
attention of the entire world.

The Achille-Fould Family Chateau Beycheville is

the best example of Louis XV architecture

RMS Queen Mary, the Windsors' favorite ship

The Duchess of Windsor aboard the Queen Mary, 1950's

Chapter 2

LE SEXY CENTER CLUB, PARIS

In spite of a significant age difference, Perry and I quickly grew to be close friends. His keen mind allowed him to understand the intricacies of a modern hospital without any formal training or prior experience. He quickly understood that many of the physicians were treating the International Hospital as a "cash cow" with no regard for the long term impact on the hospital and its reputation. Being a career diplomat, Perry's instinct was to define a compromise between our position as management consultants and the root causes of the hospital's problems: the few physicians who controlled the facility and ran it as they pleased. Bob Drake had competently explained to me how there simply was no "middle ground" and that, without major changes, the hospital was headed for disaster. In a sense, I became the diplomat's diplomat as I tried to bring these two irreconcilable positions closer together.

This situation evolved rapidly as Perry and I, often accompanied by a Board member, ate lunch at the exclusive Travelers Club on the Champs Elysées. The grand palace had been built by Madame de Maintenon, Louis XIV's "favorite." It is alleged that after Queen Marie-Therese's death in 1643, Louis secretly married Madame de Maintenon. One could only imagine the intriguing and enigmatic meetings they must have had in the very rooms in which we "took sherry" before lunch and in the former living room where we ate.

I visualized the discussions which may have occurred and resulted as the former mistress exerted considerable female power over the King. Perhaps Wallis had much in common with her as the Duchess influenced another king three hundred years later. It was King Louis XIV who, when asked to describe "The State," replied: "The State? Why the State is me!" (L'état c'est moi) as well as "After me – bedlam" (Après moi le déluge).

The night of the first confrontational Board meeting with Cheek we were hosting a quite different event. It was both a high-end business meal and some after dinner "entertainment" as the Duchess later called it when our activities became public knowledge. This time it turned out to be a relatively uneventful, instant replay of what Perry and I had previously experienced with The Chairman.

A custom had developed around his Paris appearances. Upon his arrival from Washington, DC, he would plop his round the world, tourist class TWA ticket on Perry's secretary's desk. Congressmen, in those days, flew tourist class when on certain missions and Passman always coupled his French visits with trips to Indonesia; an undertaking which ultimately would lead to the biggest scandal of his career. The efficient and compliant Sheila knew that meant she had to take the congressional ticket to the central TWA office and have the Chairman upgraded to first class for the balance of his round the world trip. While this and other costly "benefits" bothered us, it seemed to my young mind that this was just "business as usual."

Five years later, in 1978, Passman ran into several serious problems. He was sued by a female congressional aid for sexual discrimination. More troublesome was his implication in what came to be known as "Koreagate." The Justice Department investigation centered on influence peddling with Tonsun Park, a multi-millionaire, South Korean businessman. In an impressive political *tour de force* the Congressman had managed to move the trial to Louisiana where a sympathetic, Baptist jury acquitted him.

I was more uncomfortable with observing the new addition to the Chairman's extravagant collection of expensive watches. On this particular visit to Paris, Passman had inquired, "Are there any new models of Patek Philippe watches?" I had been informed that this seemingly innocent question was tantamount to "Go to Patek Philippe and buy me the newest watch they have."

It was the evenings that presented the biggest challenge. This night, as was often the case, we were to eat in a private dining room on the first floor of the grand Taillevent Restaurant on the Rue Lamennais. The restaurant had recently been awarded the highest rating of all, Michelin's coveted third star. Obtaining, or losing, it was either the best or worst dream of any French restaurateur. Even before this "promotion," all Taillevent guests were treated like royalty, especially we who arrived in official Embassy cars and ate in the elite Guimet private dining room. This exquisite room had been the bedroom of the first owner of the palace, The Duke de Mormy, before it became the Embassy of Paraguay. As usual Perry included other sympathetic, patient and enabling Board members when we were entertaining The Chairman.

As dinner progressed Passman became louder with each cocktail and glass of wine. In the absence of women, his sense of humor was vulgar in the extreme. On returning from the men's room and, probably envisioning what was to follow, he yelled, "The door says pussy but there were none!" The French word for "push" is "poussez" from which Passman had discovered his joke.

Some minutes later when a very polite, bi-lingual waiter asked if he would like some water, Passman shouted, "Water? Hell no, young man, fish fuck in water."

We all tried to create a sound resembling laughter and to redirect the conversation towards the conservative Democrat's favorite topics: his positive feelings about the Viet- Nam war and his contempt for President's Kennedy's brain child to breed goodwill around the globe, the Peace Corps.

"That jerk really believes that these young kids can be sent around the world and have a diplomatic influence on different cultures!" he exclaimed.

The seventy-five year old Congressman had been a House of Representative Freshman at the same time as Richard Nixon and John Kennedy. He had boldly deserted his fellow party member, President Harry Truman, in 1948 by walking out of the Democratic National Convention in Philadelphia accompanied by another southern segregationist: Strom Thurmond.

After the multi-course, beautifully served dinner we were off to the show at one of Paris' famous cabarets: The Sexy Center Club. It was located on the infamous Rue St Denis near "Les Halles," the market district of Paris. The street contained numerous sex shops and cabarets including Passman's favorite – where we were destined to spend the late evening. It is estimated that there are 50,000 working prostitutes in Paris and, judging from who was around that evening, the figure may be an understatement. At least one hundred women roamed the three block area around The Sex Center as we arrived and were cramped together at a small table right under the stage. While the room filled with tourists and wealthy Frenchman eager to see the well-choreographed show, bottles of Scotch and Champagne were positioned in front of us. Before the show began, Perry gave me a nod which I fully understood.

Passman had a "special" dancer friend named Michelle who he liked to "visit" after the performance. One of my tasks was to find her backstage and make the necessary arrangements for the Chairman's finale. As usual, Michelle was happy to see me but her smile soon turned into a frown:

"Non René, I will not have that old friend of yours to my apartment after work. I don't care how important he is to you," she said adamantly.

"But why?" I asked innocently, immediately regretting the question.

"I swore last time it would never happen again."

"Michelle please," I begged trying to be subtly flirtatious.

Although I might have enjoyed continuing a discussion, the moment to begin the performance was near. I could not imagine what I would say if I had to return to the table with bad news.

"Michelle," I pleaded. "I will double the 500 Franc fee (roughly equivalent to $200) if you do this one last time. I promise I won't ask you again." This would have to be my "final offer" as Perry had given me 500 Francs for the errand and I only had another 500 Francs in my own wallet. Michelle was definitely interested in the high fee.

"I'll tell you what," she conceded. "I'll do it on one condition."

Several horrible scenarios raced through my mind including that I would have to attend the festivities. Luckily for me the concession was far less personal.

"You will wait in the street below my building until he is….. finished. When this happens – and trust me it will not take long – I will flash the lights. Then you will come and get your boss and take him home. Last time, he fell asleep and I was unable to get rid of him. Can you imagine that?"

I returned to the table, took my seat next to Perry and whispered into his ear, "You owe me an additional 500 Francs and I will need your help afterwards to carry him out of her apartment. That was a *sine qua non* for the deal."

The spectacle was an *avant-guard* sex show with beautiful, sexy women straddling ropes and humping vertical bars. There were several semi-gymnastic exhibitions involving numerous women all together. All eyes were riveted on the tiny stage as the heat in the room intensified. When the lights came on Perry informed me that he would leave with the other men by taxi and I would take our guest to Michelle's in the embassy Cadillac limousine. The driver, a strong marine, would wait with me in the car until we had to perform our own gymnastics and remove Passman from the small flat. By the time we exited the club, The Chairman was barely able to stand and I wondered if he would even be able to enjoy the 1,000 Franc treat.

Whether Michelle was correct or my conversation with the marine chauffeur had my full attention I cannot say. But what seemed a negligible time later, the lights in the apartment flashed several times. We ascended the four narrow flights of stairs to find Michelle at the open door in a pink silk bathrobe. "I told you. He is passed out in the bedroom. Now it's your turn. Get him out. Au revoir!"

As the marine and I dressed the Chairman I understood the expression "a picture is worth a thousand words." There was the famous Congressional Chairman spread out in all his not-so-attractive glory, snoring. Stifling laughter, the marine and I helped him dress and almost carried him back down the stairs and laid him down in the back seat of the car. Then we drove him to the Hotel de Crillon, on the Place de la Concorde, almost adjacent to the American Embassy and brought him up to his suite. The living room looked very similar to the private dining room we had eaten in at Taillevent several hours earlier. Its dark wood paneling framed a beautiful pink marble fireplace. The décor matched the Louis XV style of the building. It had been constructed in 1758 and was owned by the Tattinger family. I could not help but to admire the beauty, even under the odd circumstances.

After depositing Passman, fully clothed, on his own queen sized bed next to another fireplace in the bedroom, the marine and I stood side by side in the brown marble bathroom and laughed as we washed our hands in double sinks.

Chapter 3

PATRICIA

"Please join me for drinks," said Perry the day after the Passman dinner. "Eighty-four Avenue Foch, ground floor right," Perry was using an elegant way to describe the location of the luxurious apartment the Embassy had assigned to the Culley's as Chief of Mission and full-time President of the International Hospital. One entered a courtyard through a porte-cochère which also had access to the two garden apartments in the building. Perry's, obviously, was on the right.

The wide, chestnut tree lined boulevard is one of the five main "avenues" which lead from the Arc of Triumph, called the star, "l'Etoile" in French, because of the large streets which, when seen from above, make the Arc of Triumph appear to be the center of a star. Eighty-four Avenue Foch and the two adjacent buildings (eighty-two and eighty-six), while beautiful, had a checkered past because they served as the headquarters for the Gestapo during the German occupation of Paris in the Second World War.

The street is often thought of as *the* address in Paris, rather like Sutton Place in New York City. It was named after Ferdinand Foch who was France's greatest general during the First World War. He also served as Supreme Commander of the allied armies. Foch became "Marshal of France" following the "Grand Offensive" in September of 1918, which expedited the end of the war. It was he who accepted the

German surrender two months later and was the main French author of the Treaty of Versailles working with the American President, Woodrow Wilson. Foch died in 1929 and is buried next to Napoleon at Les Invalides.

After the Treaty of Versailles was signed he made the most prophetic statement of the twentieth century, "This is not a peace," he said. "It is an armistice for twenty years." Of course, much of Europe and later, America, would be back at war with Germany two decades later.

After entering Perry's apartment and being seated in a cozy den off the main living room, we discussed the sad news that Alexander Onassis had been killed in an airplane accident. Alexander was my age and had been enrolled in the same Swiss boarding school as I in the late 1950's. Because his mother could not comply with the visitation rules, his tenure there was extremely brief. His death would have a major, direct effect on me fifteen months later at the International Hospital when his father, Aristotle Onassis was admitted.

Finally, my new friend and accomplice began what, clearly, was the reason he wanted to see me and was, for him, a difficult discussion.

"You know," he said, "that I have been married to Harriet for twenty-five years?"

"I did not know how long but assumed you had been young lovers during the war," I answered wondering where the discussion was going.

"Harriet and I met right after the war," he corrected me. "We had wonderful adventures at numerous embassies. But lives change course – as did ours. I fear we will soon separate." Perry paused as if he expected some encouragement.

"I am sorry, Perry. I assume that must be lonely," I said.

"Not exactly," he said sporting a boyish grin I had come to know and like. "I have fallen in love with an incredible woman and will marry her. The trouble is that my position is so damn visible and political! What makes it worse is that everyone knows and likes Harriet in our diplomatic and social circles here. She is the perfect wife at cocktail parties and, as the news gets out, I will be described as a villain, even hated."

"Should you not just face it head on?" I inquired with my young thoughts.

"Oh, God no," said the consummate gradualist and diplomat. "This has to be handled very gently, eh, *very gently*. In fact, my friend, you know the girl."

"Really?" I inquired.

"It's Patricia Sewell."

"You lucky old dog," was all I could say through my shock.

Patricia was a senior British nurse at the International Hospital. She was spectacularly beautiful: tall and slender, perfect white skin and a classic face framed by silky, thick dark brown hair. Her piercing aquamarine eyes sparkled as one was introduced to her lively spirit and remarkable charm. I had been quite mesmerized by her beauty and noticed that no male employee or physician at the hospital could pass Patricia without staring.

"She lives on the Rue de Longchamps near you," he added.

"Of course!" I exclaimed. "How stupid of me. I've seen your car parked on the sidewalk at lunch time with the flashers going."

Perry had a large sign which read "L'Hopital International" (The International Hospital) on the dash board and diplomatic license plates. He could get away with parking on the sidewalk!

"I wondered what you did there, but felt it was none of my business."

"Well, it is now. In fact, I'd like your help."

I was deeply indebted to Perry. He had selected our firm for the prestigious job. He knew how dependent the Rosemort Group was on prompt (even early) payments which he approved and, most importantly, I deeply liked the man. I also knew he would assist us during the ongoing battle with the Chief of Staff, albeit in his gradualist fashion.

"What can I do? How can I help?" I asked.

"I'd like to…. let's call it 'promote' Patricia. She writes well and has a keen mind."

I think Perry caught my smile and returned it.

"I want her to start a newsletter for the International Hospital. There is ample space in the office adjacent to mine. I just want to make sure I have your support and discretion."

After our "collaboration" with Otto Passman this was what we now call a "no-brainer." I was happy to be supportive. Plus, the idea had sound merit and I was honored to be Perry's confidant. Within a week, Patricia was seated next to Perry's office in front of big picture windows which looked out on a charming garden. Every time I walked in, her broad smile lit the entire suite of offices. It was no wonder that all male visitors tended to linger at Patricia's desk before seeing Perry or me.

I soon learned what a great pleasure it was to collaborate with Patricia. In one of her first newsletters she wrote about the *fait accompli* of the infamous infection committee in an editor's note which read, "We are proposing to present a series of short articles to acquaint our readers with a number of various departments and committees concerned in the general running of the hospital. We will begin with the problem of hospital infection."

The subsequent article entitled "Hospital Infections Committee" began "A hospital must be a safe place for patients, medical staff and employees, and it is the responsibility of the infections committee to see that this is so. Our new Infections Committee is composed of members representing many of the Hospitals' departments." The article went on to name the rotating members. Jokingly, I asked Patricia to add a special note saying that we extended our condolences to Doctors Cheek and Chevalier but the "lights were now on at The International Hospital."

Shortly after Patricia filled the new position, Martin Rosemort decided to come to Paris to see how the "job was progressing." Martin had no interest in speaking with Bob Drake because the management study "bored" him. He was keen on seeing the progress of Chris' brilliantly phased construction plan. However, he was most interested in speaking with the captivating Patricia.

Miriam did not fly and had been bemoaning the fact that she and Martin had not had a vacation in some time. As a result, a typically convoluted Rosemort scheme was born: Miriam and her younger daughter would sail to France on the relatively new QE2; Martin would join them in Cherbourg, after "working" with us, and sail home with them. Miriam would never have to be on *terra firma*, mingle with strangers and she would spend half of her trip with Martin and her Glenlivit Scotch in their suite.

The day of the QE2's turn around in Cherbourg, Martin was supposed to take the boat train from Paris' beautiful, neoclassical, XIX century "Gare du Nord" straight to the docks in Cherbourg. I said my good-byes, leaving him at Patricia's desk, and went to a particularly contentious meeting with the hospital's communist union's representative. I was amused at what they might think if only they knew how some of the consultant's money was being wasted. When I returned I was surprised to see Martin still gawking at the hypnotically beautiful Patricia.

"Martin!" I said in shock. "You were supposed to be long gone. In fact, the boat train leaves in only fifteen minutes," I said looking at my watch.

"I have been trying to tell him," said Patricia with an expression that implied "but it was of no use."

I took Martin the front door of the hospital, put him in one of our ambulances and told the driver to rush as fast as he could. "Gare du Nord in fifteen minutes, monsieur? That will be hard. OK let's go!" he said.

About thirty minutes later, a clearly panicked Martin called my office to say that he had missed the boat train and asked what he should do. Miriam would be furious if he failed to show up at the ship. I called American Express, where we had a car service agreement, and urged them to pick up a well dressed, white haired man who was "freaked out" in front of the station and race him to the Cunard dock in Cherbourg. The drive typically took just over three hours while the train left Paris four hours before the ship sailed. I thought there was still hope in getting Martin out of France that day.

The next call was from the police department in Caen, a medium sized town on the road between Paris and Cherbourg. It seems that, while Martin was shouting at the driver to go faster and faster, he caused him to have a head on collision at a red light while they were trying to pass the traffic in an oncoming lane. After hearing my explanation and pleading for leniency, the police decided to put Martin in a taxi and send him on his way because, after all, he was only a passenger. The next call was from the operator on the QE2.

"Mr. Silvin," she said in the beautiful British accent that all Cunard employees miraculously had, "I have Mrs. Rosemort on the line for you."

"Hello Miriam," I said hoping for a lucky break.

"Where's Martin?" she barked.

"He missed the boat train, Miriam, and is in a car on his way to Cherbourg. When do you sail?"

"In a few minutes!" she shouted. "I have been to see the captain who tells me that the ship must leave on time due to the tide going out. He has conceded to leave a launch at the dock so that, if Martin gets here during the twenty-minute maneuver in the harbor, a sailor can bring him to the ship. Why didn't you put him on the train? You know Martin can't speak a word of French!"

I felt like telling Miriam it was not his lack of French but rather his excessive English with Patricia that caused the problem. Were it not so sad and another costly blunder which we could ill afford, I might have found the story most amusing. Instead all I could say was, "Let's hope he makes it."

At dusk, as I was getting ready to leave the hospital, Martin called to tell me that the QE2 had sailed without him. Fearing Miriam, he asked me to first call her and then book him on a flight home the following day. He would meet the ship in six days when she docked in New York. By the time I reached Miriam, she knew the news and was crying inconsolably after several stiff drinks. A very angry and dejected Miriam traveled home alone with her daughter.

The last call I took that day was from the office of the Vice President of the United States. Spiro Agnew's chief of staff told me that the Vice President was delighted to accept the mission of being Chairman of the International Hospital's U.S. Advisory Committee. He asked if the following news release was acceptable to us,

"With its outstanding reputation and long record of public service, this opportunity to be associated with the Hospital is a very real honor and one which I am pleased to accept."

The senior aide added that the "Vice President would begin to publicize the hospital and solicit contributions to pay for the new modernization and expansion program."

Five months later, Vice President Agnew resigned when he was charged with tax evasion and money laundering. Only the second Vice President in American history to resign, he was replaced by Gerald Ford. This began the rapid decline of the Nixon presidency's reputation and was instrumental in the media's desire to probe into other presidential improprieties. In a plea bargain, Agnew was fined $10,000 and received three years probation. Following this verdict, the Attorney General of Agnew's home state of Maryland called the plea bargain "the greatest deal since the Lord spared Isaac on the Mountaintop."

Chapter 4

"GRANDE DAMES" THE GALA
JUNE 24, 1973

One of Paris' big annual events was the Grand Prix week. In years past, two very different sports could earn the title of Grand Prix winners after several days of competition: live pigeon shooting and horse racing. The former was a cruel, archaic, yet very social, event which, luckily, disappeared in the 1960's. The remaining Grand Prix was horse racing. This four-daylong event culminated with many parties. In 1973, the pinnacle of the festivities was a formal dinner-dance given to benefit the International Hospital. The venue was the lovely Pré Catelan restaurant in Paris' beautiful park, the Bois de Boulogne.

The ball had been organized by another Grande Dame, Mrs. John R. McLean of Palm Beach, Florida. "Brownie" McLean had encouraged a group of horse racing aficionados to sponsor the event for four hundred guests, two hundred of which were her "intimate" friends from America, notably Palm Beach, Florida. The Duchess had agreed to serve as "honorary chairwoman" which meant that she had little to do other than to lend her influential name to the soiree and attend the gala. Her presence, and therefore the gala, would be the high point of the week and would guarantee that any invitee must be present and, ideally, contribute to the International Hospital's cause. Importantly, the evening would be Wallis' first appearance at a large social event since the death of her husband, the Duke. She was both slightly nervous and also eager for "society" to see her back in public.

Brownie's father-in-law had founded several newspapers including The Washington Post. As a result the Washington, DC suburb of McLean, Virginia was named after him. His wife, Brownie's mother-in-law, had owned the legendary Hope Diamond which was known for its size, worth and bad luck. When Wallis met the senior Mrs. McLean's plastic surgeon who boasted that he "had lifted her face three times," Wallis replied: "I'm surprised you did not lift the Hope Diamond!" The historic stone is now on display at the Smithsonian Museum in Washington, DC and had originally belonged to King Louis XIV of France. Whenever a big event needed to be perfectly planned and executed, Brownie McLean was the ideal Chairwoman. In 1973, she lived in New York and in a huge house on Palm Beach's County Road. The home was later sold to John Lennon. Brownie was loved by all; not only for her amazing parties, but also her total abstinence from the gossip which typified many of her social equals.

The Pré Catelan was designed in the French "Belle Époque" style but, from the outside, looked like the south side of the White House in Washington, DC due to a white, central circular protrusion. The party was to be held in the "Salon d'Honneur," the largest of all the dining rooms, paneled in light oak with heavy yellow velvet curtains and decorated with large chandeliers that rival those at the Tavern on The Green in Central Park. The room opens into the tented "Jardin d'Hiver" (winter garden) which always housed extraordinary floral arrangements. The inlaid wood dance floor has an elevated orchestra where, on this occasion, Pali Gezstros, Bob Martin and Raoul Zequeira performed.

In a pre-feminist wording, a Paris paper reported that "The ball was attended by U.S. Ambassador, John N. Irwin, Honorary President of the International Hospital, and H.R.H. the Duchess of Windsor, the hospital's first lady Honorary Governor who also served as Honorary *Chairman* of the Gala" (italics mine).

Whenever the Duchess requested an escort, the man came alone regardless of his marital status. At precisely the specified time, her limousine - with the Windsor's well known interwoven, deco-style, "WE" for Wallis and Edward tastefully painted on the door - picked me up at my apartment and we proceeded to collect the Duchess. American cars and limousines, along with Rolls Royce, were still "the things to have" in the 1970's before they were replaced by Mercedes or Lexus.

Wallis was a woman who got better looking as she aged because her younger, somewhat severe features, notably her large jaw and protruding chin appeared to soften. This night she looked her best; extremely elegant but somewhat frail. She wore a floor length, high waist, sleeveless white satin dress, encrusted with beads and pearls which gave it an Egyptian flavor. As usual, her jewelry was noteworthy: a diamond bracelet and earring set and diamond headband that encircled her high forehead, displayed her beautiful hair.

Before we left Le Bois, we sat together for one drink at the entrance to the library. We shared a beige satin settee under a large portrait of the Duke's beloved mother, Queen Mary. The formal, light paneled room had Wallis' signature decorations: wall mounted candelabra, at least a dozen porcelain pug dogs on one table and numerous objects d'art on every other surface. When we left, the butler, waiting at near attention in the foyer, handed Wallis a small, jewel-encrusted purse with no strap which had been placed in the front foyer near the famous "red box." As she took it, I noticed her typically perfect posture which added to her imposing presence and mystique.

We drove the short distance from the Duchess' home through the park and passed the now-closed pigeon shoot and the impressive stables where, presumably, many of the horses were recovering from their races. When we reached the imposing restaurant, two American Embassy marine guards opened our car doors as we pulled up. The reception line was in the winter garden, followed by cocktails and dinner in the Salon d'Honneur. The Duchess had been quite clear about how we would enter the room,

"I have timed our arrival so as to only have time for one drink before dinner. I do not want to stand around for long and, therefore, I have declined being on the reception line. I'll introduce you to the women you need to know. Just stick close by. I hope I make it through this," she said lamentably. "I wonder why I committed to this event but I decided it was time I be seen again." I noticed how very thin her arms were and began to see her as fragile.

Large clumps of balloons were interspersed among the candlelit chandeliers which gave the historic charm of the room a child-like appearance. Most guests were seated at long rectangular tables of twenty, while we were at one of two smaller circular head tables. As we walked into the room, The Duchess made sure that the women who had been mentioned at the Board Meeting were introduced to me. When we met Achille Fould's sister, she said, "Genevieve, I would greatly appreciate it if you would find time to talk to Mr. Silvin about the progress being made at the hospital. You remember, my dear, our discussion?"

"Yes," replied Mrs. Pray looking at me, "please join me for drinks at six tomorrow."

There was no need to ask if I were available or where they lived. An invitation by Genevieve Achille Fould was tantamount to being invited to the Elysée, France's President's residence. Her famous home was nearly as grand and its location was no secret.

During dinner, the Duchess spoke at length of their lives during the war when they served as Governor of the Bahamas. Again, she referred to her late husband as "David" which was her tender nick-name for him which she only used when she was at ease. On this evening, like so many others, I would have liked to ask her about some of the controversial activities of their lives but, I certainly did not think it appropriate. Fortunately, at later meetings, the Duchess would feel comfortable enough to reveal many of these to me.

"I enjoyed these events when David and I attended them," she said. "But now, I find them a bit tiring." Looking at me she was generous enough to add, "I have a lovely escort but still, I am a widow and going back to an empty house."

The evening was a wonderful success for the hospital both in mon-etary and political terms. The event produced over $250,000 and the newspaper coverage helped show the local Parisians that the hospi-tal was still very well supported by influential Americans. Everything was nearly perfect until the Duchess said we were leaving just as des-ert was being served.

"René, I want to leave. We shall go!"

All the men at our table popped to their feet as I pulled back her chair and escorted her out of the room. I heard surprised murmurs as we walked from the center of the "salon" to the exit. After we entered the waiting car she said, "Maxim's is just not what it used to be. I find it too crowded."

"But we are not at Maxim's," I said.

The Duchess did not answer immediately. Instead she looked tired and distant. It was the first time that I saw evidence of what had been widely rumored, namely that she was experiencing intermittent, early stages of dementia. On the short drive back to her home she finally said: "I hope you never find yourself alone, my dear. But if you should, I wish that you have a charming escort." With that she took my hand and smiled.

JUNE 25
RESIDENCE OF GENEVIEVE ACHILLE FOULD PRAY
"A SHARK TANK"

A butler wearing a white jacket and gloves opened a large door cut out of a wooden chariot entryway at the Pray residence. Genevieve Achille Fould was one of Paris' most sought after hostesses. Everyone hoped for an invitation to the family seat, the famous Chateau de Beychevelle in Médoc. Genevieve had dazzled the Franco-American community when she married a handsome, young American entrepreneur living in France. Her husband, Sam Pray, had only just joined the hospital's Board of Governors. Oddly, he was not present this evening. He was "called away to London" she said.

Doctor Cheek had wasted no time in getting to know Genevieve and used his loyal patient, the Baroness de Rothschild, to arrange the meeting to talk to her about "the young upstart."

After climbing a wide set of stairs, the butler opened a pair of wooden doors to the drawing room, stood back and motioned that I should enter ahead of him. Genevieve was seated on a white couch wearing a light blue Chanel suit and caressing a well-groomed white poodle. As I kissed her hand I was temporarily startled by an emerald solitaire ring that extended beyond the two knuckles of her ring finger. Surprisingly, the room was furnished contemporarily, mostly in all white which was in the style that Lady Emerald Cunard had made famous in London decades earlier.

"Marcel, bring us some champagne," she told the butler after I had been shown a white leather armchair. "Is that all right with you, Mr. Silvin?" she asked.

"Bien sure, Madame," (Of course Madame) I replied.

We discussed the previous night's events and the fact that we had left the gala early.

"Was Wallis taken ill?" she asked.

"Non Madame, merely weary," I answered not wishing to discuss the matter in spite of the clear invitation to do so.

"Do you have any idea of what a great love the Duchess had when Edward was first Prince of Wales and later King of England?"

"I have some knowledge of the history, Madame. My parents were friends of theirs on the Riviera in the 1930's."

"May I suggest you study Wallis and Edward's history more carefully," said Genevieve. "You need to have in-depth understanding to get some perceptive and appreciate how unique your association with Wallis is."

"Yes, Madame, I will do so," I said quite sincerely but hoping to move on the hospital matters.

"For example," Genevieve resumed, determined to make me realize my good fortune at being close to the Duchess. "Did you know she was *Time Magazine's* woman of the year in 1936, the first woman to receive that distinction?"

"No, Madame," I answered. "I did not and I do promise to do some research. May I ask what it is that has troubled you about the new management of the International Hospital?"

"The de Rothschilds asked me to consult with their physician, Sheldon Cheek, when I was ill-disposed recently," she began. "What do you think of him as a physician?"

"It is not my place to evaluate his medical abilities, Madame," I answered again carefully not taking the bait.

"Sam told me that there was an unpleasant scene at the recent meeting of the Board and that Wallis seems to have tilted the scales in your favor. Is that so?"

"Yes, Madame. Mr. Pray mentioned during…. the discussion that Doctor Cheek had revealed his concerns to you," I said. Now it was my turn to fish for information.

"Yes he did," she said. "Most emphatically I may add. It seems that he feels you have called his medical talent into question and he was deeply offended. What exactly happened?"

I watched her elegant hand pet the sleeping dog, wondering if she had heard me called "the young upstart."

"As acting lay hospital administrator, it would not be appropriate to challenge any physician's medical abilities. In America, a medical committee would undertake that responsibility." I knew from her keen eyes that she understood there were no overseeing committees in this situation. "As long as doctors qualify for local licensing and pass their medical boards, I would have no reason to question their ability," I said hoping that my charming inquisitor knew that Cheek and his few American physician friends were also exempt from all French licensing.

"But he said you accused him of recklessness. Now that I see you, I cannot imagine you making such a bold statement so close to you joining the hospital."

"Doctor Cheek and I disagreed on patients wearing identification bracelets," I explained. "I also initiated some basic medical review committees which are standard in all American hospitals. While I will see the results, I do not serve on these committees."

"Yes, Sam explained that to me. But it was Wallis who ended the argument," she repeated. "Good going!" she said laughing. "The place sounds like a shark tank. Do be careful."

"Oh, I am sure it is not over, Madame. I will heed your advice," I said as cheerfully as possible. "May I even ask for your council in the future?"

"I'd be delighted for you to come by. This whole International Hospital thing really is amazing! And you are charming."

I stayed for another glass of Champagne almost hypnotized by her beauty and immense charisma. The French word "allure" had new meaning to me.

Had I not been thoroughly briefed by Perry Culley and the Duchess, I would have thought it most odd that local personages would take such an interest in the internal politics of the hospital. But I now understood the International Hospital was more than a hospital. It was one of the seats of American power and intrigue in France. I wondered what my former fellow students at my MBA program, who were now hard at work as assistant hospital administrators around the United Sates, would think of such a quandary. Clearly what I did outside of the hospital would be of equal, if not greater, importance to what I actually did *at* the hospital. I decided that I would dedicate one day a week to lobby Board members and, as the evening had proven, their important spouses. I would ask Perry to help me with these meetings. He was the diplomatic grandmaster and would enjoy it. I would also try to expedite the creation of the French Advisory Committee; A group that would presumably be more loyal to its founders, the administration, than the hospitals' physicians.

Eventually Genevieve rang a bell and asked Marcel to "see me to the door." She had not moved anything other than her arm during my visit. I thought I had met a modern day Ingrid Bergman effectively playing the role of a Grande Dame. But this was no acting; it came very naturally to Genevieve.

"Charming," she repeated as I kissed her hand good night.

As I left Genevieve, one of her comments obsessed me:

"May I suggest you study Wallis and Edward's history more carefully," she had said. *"You need to have in-depth understanding to get some perspective and appreciate how unique your association with Wallis is."*

Chapter 5

HISTORY OF THE ROYAL INTRIGUE
(1929 – 1937)

Following their initial meeting in 1929, the relationship between the Prince of Wales and Wallis Simpson grew slowly. For one thing, The Prince had a mistress – Thelma, and Wallis was married, living with her husband, Ernest Simpson. In the early years of this phase, when Wallis spent weekends with the Prince, both "significant others" were present. These fun-filled encounters always took place at "The Fort" or Fort Belvedere – the Prince's private home outside London, away from any press. Banquet dinners, lots of alcohol and laughter followed by dancing were the main activities. During this period, and until December, 1936, the British press had a gentleman's agreement with the Royal family not to mention any stories about their private life. Since newspapers in the United States and France had no such moratorium, some English, those with friends or family abroad, were made aware of Edward's personal activities.

Edward loved the Fort and had carefully turned the shabby old building into a modern and well-decorated home. He even cleared much of the overgrown gardens himself. When he had told his father, King George V, about his plans to refurbish it several years prior, the King is said to have answered, "Why would anyone want that queer old place?" But, within two years, that "queer old place" became Edward's refuge: fully modernized, very comfortable and beautifully decorated. Importantly it was his "home" where he felt able to unwind from the duties of Prince of Wales and later King Edward VIII.

It was not until 1933 that the Prince repeatedly sent Wallis flowers. Ironically, that is the same year Adolph Hitler and the Nazi regime came into power in Germany. Until late 1937, England's official position vis-à-vis Germany was one of "appeasement" which ignored the growing awareness of Nazi aggression in Europe. Hitler's military buildup, the basis of the threat to Europe, and eventually world peace, was only observed by a few visionaries, notably Winston Churchill, who, in the early part of the decade, was a lonely voice in the desert on the subject. The Prince firmly believed that Hitler was more anti- communist than expansionist and, consequently, the best thing would be for Europe to stand idly by and allow Hitler to crush Russia. He not only held this view until the outbreak of the war in September, 1939, but he never stopped reminding his critics that, in his mind, the war had been unnecessary.

In late 1933, Thelma returned to New York to assist her twin sister, Gloria Vanderbilt, with her highly publicized trial against the Vanderbilt family in the custody fight over her daughter, "little Gloria." Three decades later Little Gloria would become Anderson Cooper's mother. In Thelma's absence, Wallis lost no time in filling the void in the Prince's life. Although Thelma returned to England in early 1934 with the immensely rich, handsome Prince Aly Khan, she definitely planned to resume her position as Royal mistress in England.

Aly Khan was in line to become the Aga Khan upon his father's death. For fourteen hundred years the vast majority of Muslims recognized the Aga Khans as the direct descendant of the profit Mohamed and over twenty million Shia Imami Muslims believe him to have inherited the prophet's divine right. Perhaps more importantly for Thelma on their ocean crossing romance was the fact that Prince Aly Khan was reputed to be one of the period's greatest lovers, capable of making love the entire night and thus pleasing his female partners over and over again. Thelma must have thought Aly already had divine powers! Years later Aly married Rita Hayworth.

On the first dinner at the Fort after Thelma returned to England, she observed an incident that immediately convinced her that Prince Edward was under Wallis' spell. When Edward reached for some food with his hand, Wallis delicately slapped his hand and ordered him to use a fork. Such an admonishment was unheard-of and, when the Prince did not react, everyone at the table understood that Wallis had replaced Thelma as Edward's mistress. Following the rapid spread of this new reputation, Wallis was invited to every party at the highest level of British society. These functions were often hosted by Emerald, Lady Cunard, the wife of the owner of the Cunard shipping line. The association with Emerald, an avid German supporter, while enjoyable would add to the belief that Wallis was, at the very least, an early Nazi sympathizer. During this period Wallis began having many new clothes made which, presumably, were paid for by the Prince of Wales. He began to buy Wallis expensive, historic and beautiful jewelry; a collection which became legendary. Wallis' style of dress deviated from the more flamboyant fashions of the period. What later became known as the "Wallis look" was more subdued with soft colors on a somewhat severe couture. Her famous evening gowns were timeless in their simplicity and elegance.

The aging King George V's health declined during the last half of 1935, as international pressure to sanction the burgeoning threat of German aggression gradually began to grow. German rearmament had clearly begun and Germany started to recruit an army; both acts in clear violation of the 1919 Treaty of Versailles signed after World War I. These actions caused the Council of the League of Nations to sanction Hitler and thus began a growing desire to isolate Germany diplomatically. Hitler then cleverly decided to send an appeasement signal of his own by declaring that "The German Government has the straightforward intention to find and maintain a relationship with the British people... which will prevent for all time a repetition of the only struggle there has been between the two nations."

Hitler had a dual strategy of calming international opinion and concern about Germany's rearmament and then re-testing the waters by further building his military strength and violating the punitive conditions imposed on Germany after the First World War. For example, during 1935, Hitler began discussions to build a new Navy but calmed British fears by suggesting a treaty between the two countries to keep the proposed new German Navy at 35 percent of the size of the British Navy. By midyear, Hitler's new Ambassador to England, Joachim von Ribbentrop, while charming and gallant, declared that the proposed 35 percent figure was "nonnegotiable." The British never contested Hitler's position which would set the precedence for Germany to continue violations of the Treaty of Versailles by reoccupying the industrial rich Rhineland and invading Austria.

Meanwhile, Wallis and many other members of London's high society wasted no time in befriending Count von Ribbentrop. It was even rumored, probably unfairly, that Wallis had an affair with the Count who, at the time was the toast of British society. He attended functions with the always-repeated mantra that the German National Socialist party had no expansionist desires or strategies. Whether Wallis and the Count had a lover's liaison or not, the very visible and obvious friendship did not help Wallis' reputation during a year when anti-German sentiment began to grow exponentially. In fact. it created the start of the long held, unkind belief that Wallis was passing secrets to the potential enemy.

It was during this period when Wallis secured her control over Edward's royal households by firing certain long tenured servants and altering some of the remaining staff's usual customs. The couple did indeed enjoy dancing "well into the night" and upon their return to Edward's homes, they would ask staff to prepare and serve very late suppers. To add to her pleasure, Wallis also hired the head chef at her favorite restaurant: Maxim's in Paris.

In late 1935, Edward summoned Ernest Simpson and made a private deal with him to not contest divorce proceedings so that Wallis would be free to marry.

After having lived such a meteoric rise in her "station," many felt Wallis believed that she could soon become Queen. While this was ill-informed, no one could possibly have imagined the turmoil of the following two years in England and the rest of the developed world.

Fort Belvedere after the renovation, including swimming pool
and tennis court.

The Prince of Wales and Mrs. Simpson vacationing
in France. Aunt Bessie Merryman, laughing.

Thelma, Lady Furness with her twin sister Gloria Vanderbilt, circa 1933

Wallis Simpson – the Royal mistress circa 1935

FROM PRINCE TO KING TO DUKE
1936

Edward started off 1936 as Prince of Wales but on January 20th his father, King George V, died and the Prince of Wales became "Edward Albert Christian George Andrew Patrick David, King Edward VIII of the United Kingdom, Great Britain and Ireland and Emperor of India." The official proclamation took place on January 22, 1936, the same day that Edward was informed of a shocking blow. His late father, King George V, had left his entire estate to his other children and nothing to his oldest son. This new king would have to rely completely on the income from his duchies which, while not inconsequential, was a huge disappointment. Edward preoccupied himself with conflicting concerns: personal finances, international relations with Europe and his growing obsession with Wallis. Concurrently, he was furnishing Wallis' new home with treasures and artwork while buying the most magnificent jewelry for her. He also had some new pieces of jewelry made from Royal stones which would later cause a fury when the couple, and the jewels, would leave England.

At the same time, Europe gradually slipped further toward war. On March 29, 1936, Hitler called for a referendum so that the German people could vote on The Fuhrer's proposal to invade the demilitarized industrial Rhineland. The ninety-nine percent vote favoring this action essentially signaled that Germany was permanently and materially rejecting the Treaty of Versailles and had embarked on a clear course of action to significantly build a military, thus strengthening herself.

Noblesse Oblige

During the summer of 1936, King Edward borrowed one of the world's largest and most luxurious yachts, the Nahlin, and invited several guests to accompany him on a Mediterranean cruise. Although Wallis had vacationed with Edward in both the summers of 1934 and 1935, this holiday was distinctly different in two ways. First, Edward was Britain's monarch, not "merely" the Prince of Wales and second, Wallis was more of an equal partner to the King instead of "just" an invited guest.

At several stops during both the sea and land parts of the tour, Edward asked Wallis to accompany him to high-level meetings with foreign Royalty and political leaders including Turkey's revolutionary statesman and long tenured first President, Kemal Ataturk. Consequently, unlike the previous two summer trips, this highly visible vacation saw Wallis' position grow from friend and mistress to partner, political advisor and consort. At several stops, crowds understandably eager to see England's popular, handsome new King gathered to observe every detail of the exciting Royal visit.

As previously mentioned, the foreign press, unlike the British press, had no "gentleman's agreement" to abstain from covering the private lives of the British Royals. Consequently, it covered every detail of the Monarch's itinerary and meetings including the symbolic importance of his full-time companion. Within a short period of time, foreign readers of the international news were informing their British friends and relatives of their new King's activities abroad.

This confluence of events put the British press in a most difficult situation and was the impetus for the decision to advise the King the strategy of restraint would soon be altered.

During this tumultuous period, one would think that the possibility of marrying Edward would make Wallis supremely happy, but it did not. Other than the excitement at staying at the Royal summer palace at Balmoral, with the Rogers, she thought that Buckingham palace was uncomfortable and dowdy. There is ample evidence that, as the year progressed, Wallis became increasingly nervous and displeased about the mounting battle to prevent the new king from marrying her. Unlike later battles, this was not one that a young, bright but politically inexperienced Wallis enjoyed.

As European tensions continued to rise, so did the Royal preoccupation with the king's love of Wallis. Hitler was now clearly viewed as threat to peace which was worsened when The Fuhrer made an alliance with Italy's Benito Mussolini. Prior to 1936, Italy and Germany had not been allied due to their mutual and conflicting desire to control Austria and Hungary. The new pact between the two fascist dictators meant that continued peace in Europe became less and less likely. To complicate matters for Wallis, the Italian dictator's son-in-law and new foreign affairs advisor was none other than Wallis' lover of some fifteen years prior while she lived in China: Count Ciano.

The British Foreign Office began constant surveillance of Wallis when her close friend, Baron von Ribbentrop, replaced the German Ambassador to England, Prince Otto von Bismarck. In October, 1936 Wallis moved to the dreary, small, port city of Felixstowe so that her divorce could be heard, as the courts in London were backlogged. This plan was conceived to accelerate the waiting period she would have had in London and to avoid any public attention the proceedings may have created in the capital. In the days before "no fault divorce" some cause for incompatibility had to be proven. After a brief hearing with testimony from a housekeeper who claimed to have seen Ernest in bed with a lady other than Wallis, she was granted her divorce from Simpson citing "infidelities." The same evening, King Edward secretly drove his Buick himself to Felixstowe and placed a magnificent twenty-karat ring on Wallis' finger. (Historians differ on whether the ring was a diamond or a sapphire) Given that the divorce decree would not be final for six months, the King began dreaming of a June, 1937 wedding. The divorce was grated as "nisi," a Latin word for "unless," which means unless the court has future evidence of improprieties or prior relationships. This "condition" would cause both Wallis and Edward severe problems the following year.

Shortly after the divorce decree, Wallis began receiving death threats. Her nervous condition mounted and she thought of escaping England to America. At this point she "only" hoped to eventually return as "Royal mistress" rather than Queen. However, her lover, the King, would hear nothing of such a compromise.

In early December, after a rock was thrown through Wallis' window in London, she reconnected with her old friends, Katherine and Herman Rogers. She made plans to leave England and move into their Villa Lou Viei in Cannes, France. The move was expedited a few days later as a result of headlines in the British press entitled "The King and Mrs. Simpson" which included pictures of the romantic couple vacationing aboard the yacht Nahlin in the Mediterranean the previous summer. After an emotional farewell to the King, Wallis left in a fascinating, paparazzi chase escape by car to the south of France. Edward had arranged for Wallis' own car to be loaded onto a channel ferry while his close friend, Lord Perry Brownlow, and Wallis fled in Brownlow's Rolls to avoid detection. There are reports that Lord Brown-low instructed the driver to stop on the road while still in England whereupon Brownlow tried to convince Wallis to give up the King and travel to America instead of France.

Once the group (including the chauffeur and a detective) arrived in France, they switched to Wallis' car which customs officers identified as Wallis' due to the registration being in her name. A cry of "voila la dame!" (here is the lady) was heard at customs. The car and its license plate (CUL 547) soon became world-famous and the press began to follow the trip. The first "night" was a stop in Rouen at 3AM. After only a few hours rest, a beautifully dressed Wallis descended into the hotel's lobby. The area was full of reporters trying to take pictures while the detective and police tried to prevent them from doing so. A few hours later the group stopped for lunch in Evreux. The only available phone was in the hotel's bar where Brownlow placed a call to "Mr. James," the King's code name. Due to bad connections and with local phone operators listening in, Wallis tried desperately to shout instructions to her lover about what to do and who to consult. She read a list of names she had written down as comically, in retrospect, Lord Brown-low and the British detective tried to drown out Wallis by shouting at each other in front of the phone booth! Given that a Paris newspaper reported Wallis' maid and luggage had arrived in France headed for Cannes, the number of reporters increased. Finally, the famous group ran out of the hotel and began a race with the reporters headed for their next stop. In the car, Wallis realized that she had left her hand-written notes in the phone booth. While terrified about what the reporters would do with them, they decided not to turn back but to carry on to Blois, in the Loire Valley. Sadly, on arrival, they found the hotel lobby full of even more reporters.

That night Wallis and Brownlow slept in adjoining rooms with the door open so that Lord Brownlow could come to Wallis' defense in the event of a break-in. In his memoir Brownlow described the events in some detail, adding that Wallis began to tell him how "the whole thing really happened." Unfortunately, the exhausted Brownlow fell asleep only to wake up some time later to hear Wallis say "you must admit I've been very candid with you." He never heard the details Wallis was willing to share with him about the royal love affair.

The next stop was at the world famous Chez Point restaurant in Vienne, near Lyon, France where – once again – the group was met with cries of "voila la dame!" After Madame Point served Wallis and Brownlow lunch in a private dining room, Wallis crawled out of a bathroom window and jumped into her waiting car as the chauffeur tore off, deceiving reporters who were not as sophisticated then as they are today.

Several hours later and hiding under a blanket on the floor of the car, she reached her friends in Cannes late on December 7, 1936 thoroughly exhausted and dejected. By now both Brownlow and the pressures of the intrusive reporters had brought Wallis to the realization that she should give up the King. Once again, the new monarch would hear nothing of it and was adamantly determined to find a solution, however drastic, and to marry her. It was clear that Edward simply could not live without her. His insecurities vanished when he was around her and her personality and charismatic temperament was more important to him than the English throne, his family's approval or the British Cabinet's opinion.

During Wallis' harried race across France, King Edward had consulted a disapproving Prime-minister Baldwin who, in turn, consulted the Cabinet, the Church of England and even the distant English Dominions. The manner of his communication clearly led all parties to agree that a marriage to a soon-to-be twice divorced American was out of the question. If the King was truly adamant about his plan, he would have to step aside. Initially it was inconceivable that such an unprecedented action could happen, but it soon became apparent that Edward was ready "to go" in spite of advice from Winston Churchill who recommended Edward delay any decision as well as from phone calls with Wallis who used the refrain "Fight, David, fight!"

Meanwhile, as that fateful first week in December, 1936 drew to a close, the British government became increasingly paralyzed with endless discussions and meetings about the King's private life. At a time when a concentrated effort to develop a new foreign policy was crucial, much of Parliament, the Cabinet and the Royal family's concern was focused on the King's proposed marriage. The situation soon turned into a constitutional crisis with all sides refusing to compromise while groups of protesters gathered in the streets of London shouting "Marry whoever you like!"

For a brief moment, it looked as if a compromise could indeed be reached. The influential owner of the powerful Daily Mirror Newspaper came up with the concept of the King and Wallis entering into a "morganatic marriage." The term comes from Latin and means "morning gift." It was an infrequently used "solution" for a high-ranking Royal that wished to marry a low level aristocrat or, worse, a commoner. Its most famous use was when Empress Marie Louise of France, Napoleon I's widow, married a "simple" count. Importantly, it asserts that the Royal titles as well as Royal revenues cannot pass down to any child such a union may produce. Of course, no party to the deal knew Wallis could never conceive especially given the fact that she was now forty-one. The creative, suggested solution was considered by the British government, rejected by them and, even more importantly, by the Church of England. The latter refused the compromise because the thought of England's King, also the head of the Church of England and "Defender of the Faith," marrying an un-baptized, twice-divorced woman was quite simply unthinkable. The idea of a morganatic marriage was scrapped.

At the same time the Royal family was going through its own crisis. Edward had been raised from his earliest childhood to become King. The next person in the line of succession was his brother, Albert, The Duke of York. Albert was shy, physically weak and suffered from a severe stammer. He had no charisma which, when Edward was going to be King, did not matter. However, now faced with the very real possibility that he would replace his brother on the throne, the family – notably the Duke and Duchess of York – was deeply distressed. They had not been prepared for the huge responsibility, were relatively unsophisticated in matters of foreign relations and lived as private a life as was possible for members of the Royal family. King Edward and the Duke of York's mother, Queen Mary, was equally distraught at the idea which was, in part, fueled by the Duchess of York's deep hatred of Wallis. Within a short period of time, the Duchess of York would become Queen Elizabeth (not to be confused with her daughter, bearing the same name, and who, in 1952, became England's monarch as Queen Elizabeth the Second.)

None of this chaos altered the King's plan. He would marry Wallis regardless of any pressure from family, government or church. The issue had also become one of young versus old, citizens and workers versus upper class British. Demonstrations now erupted all over the country as young workers chanted "we want Edward" and workers repeated the chant of "marry whoever (sic) you like." These were difficult financial and political times in England made all the more frightening by clashes of fascists and anti-fascists in November and December.

Meanwhile King Edward met with various authorities, especially Winston Churchill, to help him understand how an abdication should be handled and what his personal finances would be after such a change. They tried to imagine as many details as possible to negotiate his finances and new title. Henceforth, he would be known as Edward, Duke of Windsor. Unfortunately, no one thought of securing Wallis' future status and whether or not, as the wife of a former king, she would be considered a member of the Royal family and therefore entitled to be addressed as "Her Royal Highness."

Finally, Edward made plans to embark on a self-exiled life in Austria until the six month period necessary to make Wallis' divorce official had elapsed. He had been advised, if he met with Wallis before such time, her final divorce decree might be withheld. The King called upon his friend Baron Eugene de Rothschild and his American wife, Kitty, to stay at their castle, Schloss Enzesfeld, near Vienna.

On December 11, 1936, King Edward abdicated the throne. He executed a document of abdication (dated the previous day) and delivering an historic radio address to the nation from a radio station in Augusta Tower, at Windsor Castle, wherein he made the famous comment "I cannot undertake the heavy burden of state without the love and support of the woman I love." Immediately after the address, the new Duke was rushed to a waiting navy ship, The Fury, to take him to France and then he traveled with secretaries, bodyguards, Wallis' favorite dog Slipper and servants to Austria.

Back in Cannes, France Wallis was uncomfortable at the aging Villa Lou Viei. She had grown accustomed to "the Royal treatment" in London. Now she had to be careful about walking in the garden or even appearing at windows as reporters were always ready to photograph the person who had become the most infamous lady in the world. People wanted to read every possible detail, no matter how minute, about this woman for whom the king of England had given up the throne. Her nerves were frayed and she became irritable as the feeling of isolation and captivity grew. Her entire life had been spent being spirited, jovial and entertaining. Everyone she had come in touch with liked and enjoyed her company. Suddenly she was being portrayed as a conniving woman in the world press. Hundreds, if not thousands, of letters arrived - most of which were disapproving, some were insulting, and still others were threatening.

Speaking about the abdication, actress Ina Claire said, "Our dramas seem tame and uninteresting. It out-Hollywooded Hollywood. It makes Greek tragedy seem trivial." Wallis and the Rogers decided that a press conference would be helpful. In front of a dozen reporters, Wallis and Herman Rogers stood on the steps to the villa. Wallis appeared sporting a plaid sports-coat draped over her shoulders, wore little jewelry and took reporters' questions. She was described as "vivacious, a winning conversationalist and a good listener."

While the Rogers were generous and certainly very comfortable financially, winter in the cold drafty villa added to Wallis' sadness and irritability. Instead of Royal parties, her social life was limited to members of the Franco-American community on the Riviera. These included, W. Somerset Maugham, Barbara Hutton, F. Scott Fitzgerald, Gertrude Stein, Elsa Maxwell and others. The entire group of American socialites spent Christmas at Villa Moresque, Somerset Maugham's beautiful home on Cap Ferrat. Only an embarrassing, drunken demonstration by Maugham's male lover, who doubled as his "secretary," spoiled the festivities.

Wallis' temperament slowly improved during the early months of 1937 with the visit of her beloved Aunt Bessie. The reunion also coincided with a gradual reduction in the number of reporters and photographers as well as her developing plans for the immediate future.

Predictably, the Duke's stay in Austria was also not enjoyable. His mood was morose, he filled his room with dozens of pictures of Wallis, he clutched a pillow of hers with the initials "WS" and he spent endless time on the phone to Cannes. He clashed from the onset with Kitty de Rothschild who objected to his constant, expensive habits including two or three long telephone calls each day to Wallis. Even their respective dogs fought and within a few months, Kitty threatened to leave the castle until the Duke's exile was over. Edward cried frequently and lamented his horrible situation, but never once did he regret his decision; the sacrifice would eventually lead to his marrying Wallis.

By early spring, the Duke moved into a small, rented house in the Austrian town of St. Wolfgang. Before he left the de Rothschild's castle, the ever-loyal Lord Brownlow arrived from England with letters of credit for the Duke and a few prized possessions. He paid de Rothschild nine hundred British pounds (roughly $4,500) - more than the cost of a luxury car in those days - for the Duke's phone charges. An amount which shocked Brownlow who, when talking about the event, frequently said, "Nine hundred pounds for love!"

Finally the torture was drawing to a close and plans were made to rendezvous at the Chateau de Candé in France where on June 3, the anniversary of David's father's birth, the two would wed. The one hundred fourteen room, twelfth century chateau was built by Louis XII and owned by Charles and Fern Bedaux. Bedaux was at the height of his enigmatic career and was listed by *Time Magazine* as one of the five top income producers of 1934. *Time* accurately described him saying that "if a movie were made of his life, facts would have to be toned down to keep in the realm of believable." Bedaux, a world explorer, was considered the father of "efficiency engineering" and was a management consultant to numerous New York Stock Exchange companies, many of which had dealings with the new Nazi government. He gave no moral consideration to his choice of business partners which would ultimately be his downfall a few years later. Accompanied by the Rogers, Wallis moved into the chateau in April and was assured by her hostess that she, Wallis, would be mistress of the estate and could make any plans or alterations she liked in preparation for the wedding. Fern and Katherine Rogers spent much of the time in Paris so as to make the offer abundantly clear, while Wallis and Herman never left the estate.

On May 3, 1937 word came from London that the divorce was "absolute." Wallis called the Duke to inform him and added: "Hurry up!" The Duke who had been packed and waiting for several days needed no urging. He took the Orient Express train the very next day carrying edelweiss flowers which he had personally picked. He looked thin but happy when he ran up the stairs saying: "Darling, it's been so long." Indeed the exile had lasted twenty-two weeks. He and Wallis walked arm-in-arm around the chateau's grounds, ate privately and appeared blissfully happy to be reunited. In addition, Wallis and Edward were delighted with their new surroundings which were much more comfortable and luxurious than either the de Rothschild's castle in Austria or the Rogers' villa in Cannes.

The eve of the wedding brought devastating news. No member of the Royal family would attend the ceremony - as well as other information which the Duke and Duchess of Windsor would struggle with for the rest of their lives. The Duchess would never be allowed to be called "Her Royal Highness" and, as such, the insult made Wallis a second-class wife in the eyes of the Royal family. The new King knew what a shocking event this would be for his older brother, but it was a Cabinet decision that he would not contest. The "Depriving Act of 1937" was printed in the London Gazette stating that the Duke was "entitled to hold and enjoy for himself only the title, style or attribute of Royal Highness, so however, that his wife, or descendants, if any, shall not hold said title, style or attribute." Clearly, Wallis would never be considered a member of the British Royal family. Due to the fact that there was no legal precedence for this decision, both Wallis and Edward never forgave the Royal family for the insult and would resent the action, which they felt was both unfair and illegal, for the rest of their lives. It would forever be that ladies who curtsied in front of the Duchess ingratiated themselves with Edward, while those who did not were treated with cold disrespect. The same reaction was applied to anyone who did not refer to Wallis as "Your Royal Highness" which created an uncomfortable dilemma. Members of Europe's high society were now faced with a clear choice. If they addressed the new Duchess of Windsor as "Your Royal Highness," or curtsied or bowed, they would never be invited to any Royal function or to Buckingham Palace. Conversely, if they did not acknowledge the Duchess' position as a member of the Royal family, the Windsor's would never receive them. Interestingly, the Windsors' position in international high society enjoyed a meteoric rise after World War II, some eight years later. During the 1950's and 1960's it became much more "chic" to be in the Windsors' good graces than those of the rest of the Royal family. For many socialites, however, the die had been cast by their earlier decision to either acknowledge the Duchess' position or not.

Offsetting this insult, which symbolized the Royal family's position that Wallis was not truly the new Duke's wife and who would enjoy all that being a member of the Royal family entails, was the understanding by many members of Europe's haute bourgeoisie that on June 3, 1937, Wallis would become the unofficial Queen of society; especially among the Franco-American community in both France and The United States.

As the wedding ceremony began an organist played Bach and Schumann followed by Handle's march as Wallis walked in on Herman Rogers' arm. She proceeded to where the Duke stood with Major Edward (Fruity) Metcalfe, the best man. Ralph Martin described the scene saying, "Wallis' gown touched the floor. Her 'something old' was a piece of antique lace stitched into her lingerie; 'something new' was a gold coin minted for the coronation of Edward VIII, with his profile, which she put in the heel of her wedding slipper; 'something borrowed' was a handkerchief from Aunt Bessie; and 'something blue' was her wedding dress." The Duke was in a morning suit and appeared both at ease, happy and to be enjoying himself.

After Reverend Jardine read the wedding service and the organist played "O Perfect Love." The newlyweds did not kiss, but greeted the sixteen guests one by one as each friend struggled to decide whether or not to bow and curtsy. Wallis asked Reverend Jardine to write something in her prayer book. At that point the Reverend looked at the Duke and asked how he should address the bride. Should he write the "Duchess of Windsor" or "Her Royal Highness, the Duchess of Windsor?" After an awkward moment the Duke replied, "write Her Royal Highness." During the reception, the Duke sprang to his feet to adjust a shade that Wallis asked to be lowered; the servants watched spellbound.

This would typify the way the Duke would treat Wallis for the rest of his life. A world famous psychologist on sexual behavior, Havelock Ellis, explained his view of the Duke's behavior as follows: "Due to Edward's quite boyish appearance…he is in some way different from most other men…. If Edward is slightly different than most men it may be much harder for him to find a woman who suits him than it would be for a *perfectly normal man* (Italics mine). Mrs. Simpson is evidently a very unusual woman… and seems a distinctive personality… I think it is possible for Edward to find real happiness with the woman he loves." Ellis' explanation fits well with what Edward himself had said when he was still Prince of Wales: "During twelve hours every day, I have to be what other people want me to be. The rest of the time I can be myself. If I married, I should spend the rest of my time being what my wife wanted me to be."

On display at the chateau were the interesting and extravagant gifts which had arrived from around the world, including Adolph Hitler's engraved gold box along with flowers.

While celebrities and reporters wondered whether the most famous couple in the world would be happy, the newlyweds left for a honeymoon in Austria aboard the Orient Express train which made an unscheduled stop to allow the very special, but late, VIP passengers to board a private car along with two hundred twenty pieces of luggage. One biographer claims the "Windsor's" were late because they had stopped for a picnic on their way to where the train waited!

The famous couple first stopped in Venice, Italy. Historians differ on how long and what occurred during their stop in Venice. Some say it was very brief, while others describe a few day stop-over during which they were entertained by Barbara Hutton and her Danish husband, Count Court Haugwitz-Reventlow who, most assert, included Count Ciano, now Mussolini's son-in-law, at a dinner. The reports maintain that Wallis behaved as if she barely knew her former lover, the debonair Italian Count, and David spoke wittily to him about the coronation of his brother, King George VI and Queen Elizabeth. Wallis referred to her sister-in-law as a "little Scottish dumpling."

Then it was on to Castle Wasserleonburg, a thirteenth century, forty room castle with a tennis court and a swimming pool. It is reported that they arrived with 260 pieces of luggage and the Duke carried Wallis over the threshold. In the weeks that followed, the couple took long walks together and indulged in some local hiking as they reestablished a *modus vivendi* which would become their routine for the next thirty-six years. In 1956 on the program "This Week," the Duchess explained one of her philosophies developed during their honeymoon as follows: "I believed with all my heart that married couples should, as early as possible, promise each other never to discuss a problem about which nothing further can be done.... otherwise, such a problem can well become a ghost which can haunt a marriage to the very end." In keeping with this almost Buddha-like philosophy it is believed – and confirmed by the Duchess – that the famous couple never discussed the events of December 1936; especially the abdication.

During the same interview, the Duchess went on to reveal her concept of love. "You see," she began, "I don't think love ever dies. It changes its course, it softens, it broadens. It may be blunted temporarily by a row or misunderstanding. But if it is genuine to begin with, it has a soul."

King Edward VIII and Mrs. Simpson's royal cruise, 1936 Yugoslavia

A worried and frightened Wallis aboard the Nahlin 1936

The Nahlin

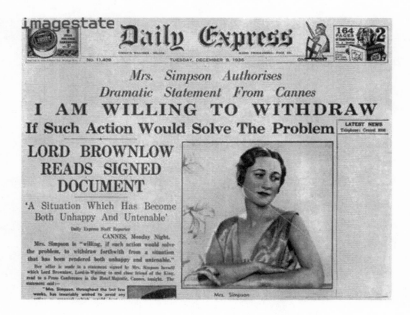

Mrs. Simpson tries to "withdraw" from her relationship with the King

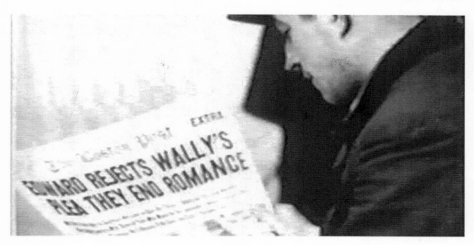

The King rejects "Wally's plea" to end the romance

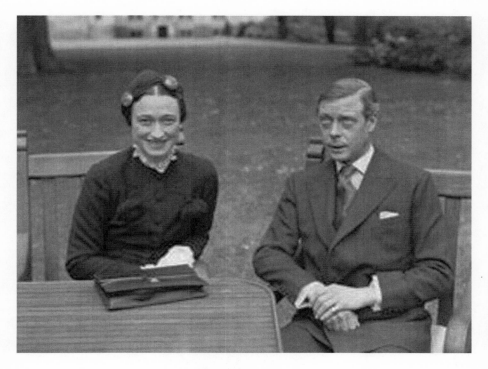

The Duke arrives

At the Chateau de Condé

May 7, 1937

June 3, 1937 The Windsor marry at the Chateau de Condé

The Windsor's wedding at the Chateau de Condé, June 3, 1937

Honeymoon in Venice June, 1937

Part Three

OTHER DUTIES

Chapter 1

UNIVERSITY OF COLOGNE HOSPITAL

Prior to the International Hospital of Paris contract, The Rosemort Group's largest and most lucrative project was with the construction department of the city of Cologne, Germany (Staatshochbauampt). The huge University of Cologne Hospital was made up of a large number of inchoate buildings scattered over several city blocks; some of the structures dated back one hundred years. In a bold decision, the city government had embarked on an eight year construction project to replace 1,000 of the 2,200 beds, group them into a new bed tower (Bettenhaus), build a gigantic, new diagnostic and treatment center and create a centralized materials handling building. It would be one of the world's greatest engineering wonders.

Through a network of underground tunnels the factory-like supply center would collect soiled materials from the multitude of medical buildings and redistribute new and processed supplies to the user departments. The edifice itself was a technological marvel as was the automated cart system that, when working properly, continuously hummed through the tunnels. The concept was the solution to incorporating some modern hospital techniques to many scattered old buildings and a few new ones. The idea was Martin Rosemort's brainchild and he loved being involved with the early planning phases of the long and lucrative project. The overall master plan would eventually reduce the total bed count of the research facility to 1,500 and add space for what has become a world famous institute on Human Genetics.

The Bed Tower was the largest suspension building in the world. A central core structure had been built which, during the early stages of the project looked like a huge, rectangular concrete tower. It contained the electrical, plumbing, mechanical and elevator shafts. Each 80-bed floor was assembled on the ground and elevated to the top of the central core. Gradually, more and more floors were erected then raised until all fifteen floors were in place, suspended from the top. One entered the hospital through the remaining visible part of the core by walking under the suspended building. The one thousand bed "Bettenhaus" had been on the cover of every major architectural, engineering and hospital journal. The two bottom floors of the tower contained medical offices and outpatient clinics. The main treatment areas, including a twenty-four room operating suite were efficiently grouped in the adjacent building which was Europe's largest and certainly its most modern treatment center.

In 1973, the construction of the mammoth project was completed and Rosemort had been awarded an additional contract to assist the local staff in opening the hospital and being present until the new beds and, more importantly, the supply and distribution center were operational. Of major concern was the automated underground cart system which, in the early days, frequently broke down or malfunctioned.

Every Thursday evening, accompanied by either Bob or Chris, depending on the current problems, I would take an evening train from Paris to Cologne's central station across from the city's beautiful Dom Cathedral. We would have a leisurely dinner in the dining car and review the areas to be addressed the following day, at the weekly Friday meeting of all the effected departments. Upon arrival into the city, we walked across the imposing square and stayed at the Dom Hotel, almost adjacent to the cathedral.

The section of the majestic, gothic cathedral closest to the train station had been damaged during the allied bombings of Cologne. Repairs were still ongoing and numerous stonecutters were working on rock outside, in plain sight of passers-by. Their artwork would eventually replace the ugly, temporary cement and plaster patches on the church's walls. On one occasion I had escorted Francis Sayre, the Dean of the unfinished Washington National Cathedral in Washington, DC, to observe the work. Using me as interpreter, Francis, who was Woodrow Wilson's grandson and bore a striking resemblance to his grandfather, spoke with the various project foremen and managers. He obtained permission to have some of the talented and nearly extinct German stone masons sent to America as soon as their mission in Cologne was completed.

The project started off with a positive relationship between the city officials and Rosemort. However, the goodwill had deteriorated and our meetings were often confrontational and acrimonious. The basis of the discord was the disparity between what Martin had alleged regarding the automated transportation system and the actual state of its operations. When carts would break down in tunnels or dedicated elevator shafts, a chaotic situation took place: people pushing carts down crowded streets, frantically trying to deliver loaded carts to various buildings, often during inclement weather. Meanwhile, soiled supplies were being hurriedly returned to be processed. Other employees were dispatched into the tunnels to remove the damaged carts and repair the overhead conveyor system. Some Fridays

131

I would enter the supply building to find as many as thirty damaged carts crowding working areas and numerous angry and confused employees.

Every Friday evening we would report to the city officials accompanied by the hospital administrator and the department heads affected by the problems. The once positive and productive gatherings had gradually become anxious moments which were made worse by the fact that discussion would last well into the night until everyone was both exhausted and frustrated. Usually, I would return to Paris on Saturday unless I had conceded to work with department heads over the weekend.

An additional issue exacerbated the problem. The Rosemort Group's financial health in America was deteriorating, so I needed prompt payments from both Paris and Cologne. Without these funds the debts mounted and the consultants in Washington were not paid on time. The resulting sad state of affairs produced a dwindling staff plagued by deteriorating morale. Martin's once highly respected, sixty person consulting and architectural staff had fallen to thirty disgruntled professionals, most of whom were incapable of securing different positions like their departed colleagues already had. At least once a week I would have an almost identical conversation with the Rosemort financial officer in Washington, DC.

"Payroll will be due next week and we are about $50,000 short," Lee would say.

"We send back at least $25,000 net of our expenses each week!" I would remind the competent yet highly stressed accountant.

"If you cannot add some more by Monday, employees will have to forgo their salaries. We have been cut off by various suppliers and numerous creditors are calling all day long."

My thoughts were taken back with horror to the creditors' calls I used to receive before the Paris contract had saved my mental health by allowing us to move overseas. I reminded myself that the person on the other end of the line, Lee Willis, was having a much worse day than I. My remote location removed me from the day to day financial concerns in Washington in spite of being responsible to repatriate a large percentage of the firm's operating income.

Week after week, I either appealed to Perry in Paris or the much less sympathetic city officials in Cologne to approve an interim bill with an immediate payment. On one occasion, I chased the comptroller of the city of Cologne through a cold, damp train station trying to get him to approve and sign an invoice so that, in his absence the following day, I could get a check and wire the funds to Washington. Sadly, it was a never-ending situation which put my team and me at a severe disadvantage in trying to be professionally responsible in the fulfillment of the contractual duties.

One day, while back in Paris, I received a call from Lee. "This may well be the end," he said.

"What's wrong now?" I asked.

"The regular quarterly payment from Cologne has been frozen."

"But, I got that approved when I was there just the other day," I said confused.

"It's not the city which is holding it up. It's the tax authorities who have blocked the city from paying us. It seems that they want to apply the value added tax for all eight years of payments."

Germany used a controversial "VAT" (value added tax) system, which taxed all work and supplies at each stage of completion. We had repeatedly been advised by Arthur Andersen, our accountants, that, as long as the reports and drawings were prepared outside of Germany and delivered to Cologne we were not subject to the tax. We knew that, as consultants, we were operating in a grey area but the matter had never before reached the level of freezing our receivables. The cumulated tax liability would be greater than the remaining balance of our payments for the project which would certainly mean bankruptcy for Martin, disgrace for his family and the end of the company.

It was ironic, I thought, as I had discussed these financial issues with The Duchess over dinner at Maxim's. People who knew her from afar would never guess that she could be remotely interested in the construction of a new University Hospital in Germany much less in my financial problems and collection methods. But the Duchess I knew was not only willing to listen but was also eager to hear details of this life she had not known. It proved how keen her mind still was and how generous she was to a young protégée.

She loved eating at Maxim's in a formal dinner dress and, therefore, I wore black tie. The dinner meetings had become a monthly ritual and I was always surprised when her assistant called to schedule the appointments. I assumed that Wallis would tire of the events but, instead, she seemed to genuinely enjoy them. She listened carefully to my perhaps naïve and youthful descriptions of my career. Within a few months everyone at Maxim's expected us to appear together and bowed, after groveling before the Duchess of course, most of the women curtsied; men bowed.

One evening I told her about chasing the official from the City of Cologne through a train station so that he could approve a bill we needed paid.

"Do you mean to tell me that you have to run around begging for money in Germany?" she asked laughing one night as we were seated. "And begging bureaucrats, en plus?"

"Yes, Duchess," I replied. "It is a matter of financial life and death to my in-laws. It's part of what I do."

"And you spend time with that wretched Deberry chap?"

"Yes, Duchess, we think he will build a hospital and we will design it."

"Such tedious people do not deserve this service," she said almost annoyed. "Remember, René 'no good deed goes unpunished,'" she said smiling. "I hope you do not have to learn this the hard way. You have what I call 'sparkle' now, René. That will vanish with the years – with life's travails. Trust me it does not last. Do not waste it. Your mother had it when she was young. In fact I admired her."

"You admired mother, Duchess?" I asked visibly surprised. "Why?"

"Well she was younger than I but that's not it really. We were both struggling to learn French and your mother managed to make it fun to listen to her. I was embarrassed about my accent and she made it work to her advantage. She could make a room full of stuffy French-men laugh with her when she made an error by saying 'I know I speak French like a Spanish cow.'" Neither Wallis nor the Duke were ever able to master French. Although the Duchess' French was better than that of the Duke's.

The Duchess then took on a distant and absent look which I had begun to see with increasing frequency. The waiter who was permanently assigned to our table when we ate at Maxim's was looking at us, wondering if he could be of service.

"Now, let us order and not speak of difficult subjects again this evening. I am weary," she said nodding her head by a tiny millimeter to inform the staff we were ready. Then she gently tapped her empty Champagne glass with her index finger indicating that he could pour some more.

Throughout the dinner Wallis reminisced about their lives and their travels. The experience is so complicated that the reader may appreciate a brief history of their married lives.

University of Cologne Hospital 1,000 bed tower under construction.
The completed structure will be the world's largest suspension building.

The author (left) working with German architect in Cologne

Maxim's restaurant, Paris

Chapter 2

THE DUKE AND DUCHESS' WAR YEARS
1937 — 1945

During the first years of their marriage, Wallis developed a pattern of behavior which was uniquely crafted to be of service to her husband. It was designed to make him as comfortable and secure as possible while also trying to give the former King a sense of purpose. In the words of Sir Dudley Forwood, the Duke's equerry (roughly the equivalent of a house manager and personal assistant), "…this intelligent woman…. dedicated herself to making the marriage a success. She went into her marriage with the supreme thought that this was for keeps, no matter how apprehensive she might have been."

However, neither Edward nor Wallis fully understood that their involvement, in any form of international affairs, was over after Edward's abdication. They hoped to be of value and use to Britain. The British government felt quite differently and still had the couple under surveillance indicating a basic lack of trust for the couple's judgment. The official hope was that the heretofore influential Prince, and briefly King, would disappear and leave the matters of state up to the appropriate authorities. Unfortunately, Edward had different ideas and was overly vocal – even indiscrete on occasion – about expressing them.

It is not that Wallis and Edward were not intellectually gifted. In fact, Wallis was quite bright. Their vision was blurred, however, by what they perceived as a huge insult by the Royal family and the government's misunderstanding of how to handle Hitler. Further complicating this, they were ill-advised and as a result their activities in 1937 and 1938 – Europe's last years of peace were used against them. The transition from world peace to world war can be viewed as having existed during the first two years of Wallis' marriage. British historian A. J. P. Taylor wrote that "the watershed between the two wars lasted exactly two years. The Post-World War I period ended when Germany reoccupied the Rhineland on March 7, 1936; the pre-World War II began when she annexed Austria on March 13, 1938." The reader will remember that the Windsors' wedding was on June 3, 1937 and their controversial visit to Germany was in October of 1937.

There was a fleeting moment of false security when Prime Minister Neville Chamberlain returned from Munich on September 30, 1938 with what is known as "The Munich Accord." The letter he brandished, only three sentences in length, read "We, the German Fuhrer and Chancellor and the British Prime Minister … regard the agreement signed last night and the Anglo-German naval Agreement, as symbolic of the desire of our two peoples never to go to war with one another again." That night, Edward's brother, King George VI, made the unprecedented move to invite Chamberlain to appear with him on the Royal balcony at Buckingham Palace which attached a final royal approval on "appeasement." Little did the British royals or their Prime Minister realize that despite this accord, Hitler had already started his preparations for his "Blitzkrieg" (the original "shock and awe") of Poland which, a year later, pushed the world into war.

In October of 1937, Wallis and Edward embarked on their diplomatic tour throughout Europe which was arranged by their wedding host, Charles Bedaux. By now, Bedaux was a consultant to Hitler's new national worker's union, the *Arbeitsfront,* and promoted his concept of "speed-up stretch-out" employee management style. Along with his wife, Fern, Bedaux entertained the Windsors at their other European castle in Hungary. It is believed that it was here that the plan to visit Germany and meet with Hitler was conceived. After the prolonged honeymoon of relative isolation in "a silent castle" as she called it, Wallis was excited about the idea and argued that David was, after all, a private citizen and could travel wherever he liked. While Bedaux went to work planning the German visit, the Windsors went to Paris and set up temporary residence in a nine-room suite at the Hotel Meurice.

Bedaux was quickly able to set up the mock state visit. He was assisted by the Duke of Coburg, a grandson of Queen Victoria. He had inherited his German title while at Eton and became the head of the House of Saxe-Coburg-Gotha which had intermarried with many of Europe's Royal families. The Duke of Coburg sent a confidential memorandum to Hitler indicating that, while Edward was King, he had often said that an Anglo-German pact was all-important and that the overly punitive League of Nations was a travesty of history.

The Windsors' arrival in Germany that October had all the trappings of a state visit. They had two aircraft and eight cars placed at their group's permanent disposal. The Duke of Coburg insisted that everyone refer to Wallis as "Your Royal Highness" and thus became the first royal to address her as such which, needless to say, ingratiated him with Wallis, but especially with Edward.

Edward behaved as if he were still King and appeared unable to comprehend that there had been a fundamental change in his authority and position. He visited numerous German factories never failing to comment on how efficient and progressive Hitler's Germany was. Wallis was particularly impressed with Field Marshal Hermann Goering who, as President of the German Reichstag (German Parliament; now called the Bundestag) was a leading member of the Nazi Party, commander of the Luftwaffe (Air Force) and Hitler's successor designate. While visiting Goering's country estate, Wallis noticed a map of Europe showing Austria within the German borders. Goering is reputed to have explained the map as a futuristic work because Austria would eventually be part of Germany. Some historians claim that Edward noticed a similar map in Hitler's office a few days later.

Hitler seized the opportunity to receive the Windsors, by giving them a grand tour of Germany. Nazi salutes were given and returned. On October 22, 1937, Edward and Wallis traveled to Hitler's Alpine lodge and military retreat of Berchtesgaden aboard Hitler's special train from which they were driven up the mountain in Hitler's custom built Mercedes. Wallis stayed with Hitler's deputy, Rudolf Hess, while Edward met with the Fuhrer. Afterwards the three men and Wallis spoke for several minutes. Remembering the visit, in her memoir *The Heart Has Its Reasons,* Wallis wrote: "I could not take my eyes off Hitler." She added that he had "great inner force" and described his eyes as "truly extraordinary – intense, unblinking, magnetic, burning with the same peculiar fire I had earlier seen in the eyes of Kemal Ataturk," Turkey's dictator Wallis had met in 1936.

Hitler's appreciation of Wallis must have been similar because he is known to have said that Wallis would be a "great Queen for England."

Naturally, the British authorities' concern for the former King's behavior mounted, as did their surveillance and discussions about what could be done to curtail their meetings with important leaders on the European continent. The trip was so successful in Bedaux's mind, however, that he immediately planned an encore visit to the United States where they would tour American factories using the Windsors to draw crowds. Wallis was ecstatic about the idea of returning to America with her Royal husband and probably imagined receptions like she had experienced in Germany. Detailed plans were drawn up and their arrival in New York aboard the German luxury liner Bremen was scheduled for November 11, 1937. Forwood, the loyal equerry, wrote a seven-page letter to the captain of the Bremen outlining what orders and special requirements the Windsors would need to be provided aboard ship.

But powers on both sides of the Atlantic were working to have the American tour aborted. Sir Ronald Lindsay, the British Ambassador to the United States, was instructed to discourage the American Secretary of State from extending official invitations to the Windsor's. Together with then Under-Secretary of State Sumner Wells, a memorandum was prepared for Secretary of State, Cordell Hull, which read, in part, "The Ambassador (Ronald Lindsay) said rather significantly that there recently had been a widening of this sentiment of indignation (against the Duke of Windsor) because of the fact that the active supporters of the Duke of Windsor within England were those elements known to have inclinations towards fascist dictatorships and that the recent tour of Germany by the Duke of Windsor and his ostentatious reception by Hitler and his regime could only be construed as a willingness on the part of the Duke of Windsor to lend himself to these tendencies."

Unfortunately for Bedaux, his management concepts were now considered as usurious to workers forcing American unions to threaten mass strikes if the delegation came to the United States. Janet Flanner wrote an article in The New Yorker stating that Bedaux had been "called a Fascist in forty-eight states" and that while this did not seem to bother Bedaux, his "failure had." Bedaux had lost "...his pride; success was his natural element and vanity was essential to his state of well-being."

The combined fury was sufficient to cancel the trip on the eve of the Windsors' departure which was communicated to the Duke by Bedaux in a telegram which read, "Sir, I am compelled in honesty and friendship to advise you that because of a mistaken attack upon me here, I am convinced that your proposed tour will be difficult under my guidance."

Wallis was devastated by the cancellation of her return to America and extremely concerned for what the Duke would do in the future if he were to be removed from the public eye. Watching her husband undergo what she believed as a slow and tortuous dismembering of his self-esteem was her worst nightmare realized. But Wallis never stayed still or defeated for long. She turned her thoughts and energy to securing not one, but two grand homes, in France where she would do her best to create a regal if not royal surrounding for the two of them. In what became a trend, both houses were more or less loaned to the Windsors; this was due to Wallis' ability to get very fine objects (even homes) for little or nothing. She found a beautiful town-home on Boulevard Suchet, overlooking the Bois de Boulogne, in Paris. It belonged to a wealthy Italian who received practically no rent from the Windsors because, like so many other benefactors, he was delighted to have the former Kind of England calling his property home.

Concurrently to the Windsors moving into the house on Boulevard Suchet, Adolph Hitler invaded Austria in mid March of 1938 in what became known as the "Anschluss." Although Wallis was hard at work decorating "her" two homes the news must have brought back visions of her conversations with Goering about the map of an expanded Germany.

On the Riviera, a similar "rental" arrangement was made for a "La Croe," a lovely villa (often referred to as a "Chateau" or castle – which it is not) on Cap d'Antibes near Cannes. The ocean side of the grand white structure was built to look like a grounded ocean liner. Wallis was delighted to call La Croe "home," especially since she had previously hoped it to be the venue for their wedding.

Wallis set out to decorate both homes and to install the many antiques and art that Edward had given her during his brief tenure as King. She also prominently displayed pieces showing guests details of Edward's history as Prince and King. One room was called "the bridge" (as in the wheelhouse of a ship) where Edward's World War I mementoes from his service in the navy were cleverly exhibited. In many ways she did not want Edward – or anyone for that matter – to forget his background and yet, since she refused to speak of the abdication, she conversely did not want *him* to remember too much.

Edward's final pre-war attempt to insert himself into the world of international politics led to naught, much to his and Wallis' fury. They made a humiliating, brief and futile trip to England hoping to be met with both a royal welcome and news of an assignment for an important post for Edward. A destroyer was ordered to ferry the former King across the channel at night. Edward spent much of the brief trip talking to the captain, his close friend, Lord Louis Mountbatten, while Wallis stayed alone in an officer's cabin. To their dismay, no official welcome was offered to them as the destroyer docked and no invitation was received about an official post. Edward's brief meeting with his brother, King George VI, was a disappointment. The posts Edward wanted were denied him and the post he accepted (to be a liaison with the French army) was beneath him.

Upon their return to Paris, and with Wallis advising him, they chose Verdun, France, where the German and French armies had lost an estimated 400,000 troops during the First World War to capitalize on Edward's new position and to make a grand statement. There, at one of the famous battlegrounds, Edward delivered a radio message intended to reach the American people. In spite of the British Foreign Office's attempt to convince the former monarch not to deliver any speech, Edward did so in May of 1939, only three months prior to England's declaration of war. He began the rather innocuous address with, "I speak as a soldier who served in the Great War, all too conscious here in Verdun of the presence of that great company of dead. It is my earnest prayer that such cruel and destructive madness shall never again overtake mankind." Predictably, few felt the speech was particularly inspiring. This ambivalence led Wallis to believe that, once again, the British authorities had sabotaged the impact of the address by an inadequate dissemination of the text. She concluded that "they" would never be "motivated to solve our problems." The problem to which she was referring was offering Edward an important and visible international position.

When war broke out on September 2, 1939, Edward - once again - wanted to be given a position of responsibility. Instead, he was assigned the role of inspecting the French defenses. The task was short lived due to Edward's true, yet inappropriate, revelation to various friends, including suspected Nazi sympathizers, that the French army was woefully unprepared to face a Nazi invasion.

By early 1940, London was being bombed. Churchill, now Prime Minister, wanted to relocate the Windsors as far away and with as small of a presence as possible. In spite of Edward's hopes to become either Governor of Canada or Viceroy of India, he was appointed Governor of the Bahamas instead. Once again, the Windsors felt insulted, but as military hostilities mounted they realized that they had to flee Europe and the dangers of war.

Churchill had other worries and resented the frequent discussions with his previous friend, Edward, about his activities and his new role. The couple accepted the mission to go to the Bahamas and made their way to Spain and eventually Portugal to prepare for the voyage. These were dangerous times everywhere in Europe and it is surprising how long it took the Windsors to actually leave Europe. They finally boarded a ship in Lisbon headed first to Bermuda, having reserved ten cabins and a suite on an overcrowded vessel, full with fortunate refugees trying to escape Europe in any accommodation possible. On the first day of the voyage, the ship was buzzed by a Pan American Clipper on its way to New York; aboard the plane were Eugene and Kitty de Rothschild, the Duke's hosts during his self-imposed exile, who had arranged the event. Even while leaving Europe, during a massive crisis, it appears that the Windsors were in denial about both the gravity of the situation and the importance, or lack thereof, of their official functions.

Once in the Bahamas, Wallis was disappointed at the condition of their allocated residence: Government House. While she did her best to eventually make it more livable, the heat, sand flies and the isolation seemed unbearable. In late 1940, the Duke planned a trip to the United States, which neither Roosevelt nor Churchill approved. Consequently, after numerous discussions they were ordered to abandon the plans. However, Wallis did travel to Miami for periodontal surgery. The couple also visited the United States three times during the war years but always unofficially; received by few important figures and denied significant access to the British embassy.

It was during her years in the Bahamas that Wallis made her first foray into the world of volunteer work. Given her ability to juggle many tasks simultaneously, she undertook the role of England's diplomatic and societal queen as well as spending a few hours each day as titular head of the local Red Cross. She was also actively involved in setting up food canteens for American soldiers. One night while being driven back to their residence, she noticed a few soldiers standing in front of the Red Cross canteen looking dejected. She ordered her diver to stop the car and inquired what the soldiers were doing and what they wanted. It turned out that they were hungry and had been told they could get some food at the Red Cross. They arrived only to discover that the canteen was closed. In a typical and under-reported gesture, Wallis unlocked the door, brought the young men into the kitchen and both cooked and served them ham and eggs.

In early July, 1943 a close friend of the Windsors residing in the Bahamas was found bludgeoned to death. Harry Oakes had frequently hosted the Windsors. In many ways Oakes was similar to Wallis' other notorious friend, Charles Bedaux in that he was an enigma who had accumulated a vast fortune while frequenting less than savory friends and associates. Upon learning of the death, Edward called the Miami police asking them to fly over to Nassau to investigate "Oakes' suicide." Why Edward decided on this approach is confusing since there was no way the death could have been committed by the deceased's own hands. Wallis was unnerved but is said to have said "well, there is never a dull moment in the Bahamas!"

Oakes' son-in-law, Count Fouquereaux de Marigny, was accused, tried and acquitted. The unsolved murder was widely believed to have been the work of Oakes' business enemies who had possible ties to the Mafia. Whether or not the unpleasant experience hastened the Windsors' departure from the Bahamas is a matter of conjecture but Edward did quickly shorten his five-year commitment to serve as Governor. The Windsors permanently left their post and went to New York where Wallis and Edward spent the final war months mostly shopping, visiting friends and being the social sensation of the city. It was here that Wallis also exhibited a growing need for privacy which only added to her mystique, fame and glamour.

From New York, the Windsors made a brief stop in England where they stayed with their friend, Lord Dudley at his estate outside London. The purpose of the trip was Edward's final, unsuccessful attempt to gain an official position of importance. At Lord Dudley's, a cat burglar entered Wallis' room while she was at dinner and stole several pieces of jewelry which were insured for $600,000. Rather than being a time for celebration as the war was drawing to a successful end, the period was clouded by Oakes' murder, the jewelry theft and the scandalous reports of both incidences in the world press. Salacious rumors that Wallis was seen wearing some of the stolen jewels did not help her spirits. She began to long for their earlier, relatively gossip-free lives in France.

Finally, within days of the end of the war and after nearly six years, the Windsors returned to the Riviera, in September, 1945. Interestingly, both homes and all their stored belongings had been spared from any destruction of war and German occupation. Wallis' spirits rose when they took up residence at La Croe. They arrived with an international household staff of five, plus the seventeen year old Sidney Johnson who they had hired in the Bahamas. He would remain a loyal valet to the Duke for the next twenty-five years.

The Boulevard Suchet house in Paris had been sold but the possessions had all been carefully stored. Once Wallis was satisfied with her job of updating and bringing La Croe back up to its previous glory, she would focus her attention on replacing the Boulevard Suchet home in Paris. Before long, she would negotiate the greatest of all her grand "coups" by securing a long-term lease on Le Bois from the city of Paris.

Wallis Simpson first "Woman of the Year" Time Magazine 1936

Wallis Simpson, *Newsweek*'s cover, 1936

With Adolph Hitler October, 1937

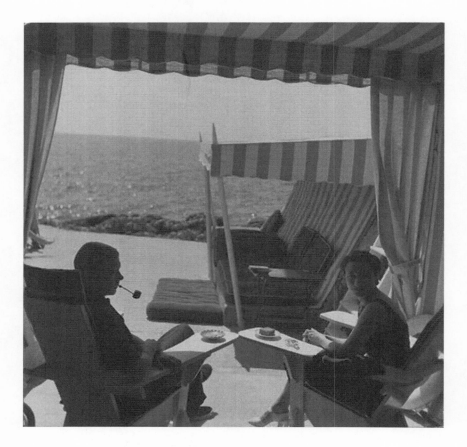

At La Croe's cabana outside Cannes, France 1938

The Duke and Duchess of Windsor at the outbreak of World War II

The Duke and Duchess of Windsor

The Bahamas circa 1942

The Windsor's at Governor's House the Bahamas, circa 1943

The Duchess of Windsor, head of the Red Cross

Bahamas circa 1943

Chapter 3

DETAINED

After my dinner with Wallis at Maxim's, I went to Arthur Anderson's Paris office to receive both an update on the tax law and to hear their opinion on the current crisis. Once again, they felt we were not subject to the value added tax if the architectural drawings and management reports were not actually prepared *in* Germany. Their recommendation was to turn our fiscal concerns over to the Arthur Anderson office in Cologne; a solution which would not only be costly but would inevitably take longer than we had.

My childhood friend, Ahmed Yehia, was pursuing a promising career at Proctor and Gamble after his graduation from the Harvard Business School. I recalled that the talented, imaginative and versatile Yehia had owned a hockey team which played in Germany and had encountered similar problems relating to whether or not their receipts were subject to the German value added tax. I reached Ahmed in Cincinnati and over the phone he introduced me to his now retired German accountant.

Heinrich Kowall lived in Bonn, Germany. Prior to his retirement, he worked for a large, international accounting firm and was clearly happy to undertake a brief and specific mission. It was apparent that he found working first with Ahmed and later with me to be fulfilling as he, an elder statesman, tried to educate and assist we apparent entrepreneurial "kids."

The cities of Cologne, and Germany's capital of Bonn, are serviced by a common airport more or less equidistant from the two urban centers. Kowall had agreed to meet my flight from Paris and accompany me to Cologne for a review of the case and to be the lead at a meeting the following day.

Luckily Ahmed had warned me that Kowall was handicapped. This information allowed me to quickly pick him out of the usual crowd that greets passengers as they exit the customs area into the main airport lobby. The man was short, slightly overweight and had a black glove-coated, metal hand, a wooden leg and a glass eye. If not so tragic, his appearance would have been somewhat comical. I quickly learned that he had been an explosives expert during the war. While trying to dismantle an allied bomb, it exploded - thus blowing off much of the right side of his body and face and leaving him with the resulting permanent injuries.

The "information age" was still a decade away so I had brought my files to review with Kowall who did not possess a telefax machine, the then-current modern information transfer mechanism. In those days, we were not fortunate enough to have the facility to scan, e-mail or fax documents. When we reached the Dom hotel, Kowall was perspiring profusely and needed a strong drink of Schnapps. I wondered if Ahmed's judgment had been less than perfect, for the first time in my long relationship with him. But my childhood pal had been clear in his warning: "Don't let his appearance or constant need for Schnapps mask his determination, knowledge and persistence," he told me after describing what the German man had achieved for him during a similar problem. "If anyone can, he'll get the job done. He is tough as nails. This is his area of expertise and you need a German to talk to the city officials as you are obviously not 'one of them' at this point," Ahmed had correctly said.

I explained to Kowall that this event could well be the difference between corporate life and death which meant that I had one, and only one, shot at rectifying what seemed like a hopeless condition. Martin had confirmed this during the several nearly panicked calls I had received from him over the preceding, rather intense thirty-six hours. The man who had always prided himself in "working well under pressure" during profitable times was clearly now coming unhinged. Martin had a terrible habit of chewing his ties when he was anxious and I wondered if, back in Washington, DC, any of his colorful ties were any longer than six inches by now!

Kowall and I spent much of the night going over our bills, collections and receivables from the city of Cologne over the years. He was visibly amazed at how much the hospital had cost and how much the city government had paid a foreign hospital consultant. Within a short period of time I was convinced that I had come across a miraculous collaborator who would fight for me with all his might. The following day we went to see the city's finance director whose offices were in the same suite as the mayor. After introductions were made Kowall began:

"Herr Zilvine," he said using the harsh German pronunciation of my surname, "or the Rosemort Company in America is not subject to local value added tax." He went on to explain what I knew and had been the rationale for our tax exemption over the previous eight years. While Kowall spoke, he pounded his metal hand on the metal desk which created a frequent loud clanging sound. The noise magnified as the meeting progressed and as Kowall's anger seemed to increase. I kept looking at the desk expecting to see dents in it.

German bureaucrats love long meetings and reviewing lots of paper, so the discussion went on for nearly two hours. I had learned that thick files were also impressive at the Staatshochbauampt and I had brought a small suitcase full of documents containing legal and accounting opinions. Around midday, the Chief Financial Officer said that he was leaving for lunch and would review the matter the following day and get back to us. In what was an amazing act of strength and hostility, Kowall pounded the metal desk with all his elderly might.

"That is unacceptable," yelled Kowall. "Herr Zilvine has a legitimate concern and an approved bill. There simply is no justification to withhold his payments. In fact, if you do not release these funds at once, I will put him in the hands of an attorney who will sue the city for damages."

The senior bureaucrat rose indicating that he was going to lunch regardless of our pressing concerns and that the meeting was over. With amazing speed the rotund, elderly Kowall sprung to his feet and pushed the metal desk backwards actually pinning the much larger man against the wall.

"You are going nowhere," he said trembling, "until we have a resolution! You are here to serve us and to behave responsibly."

Initially, I feared that we had gone too far; that the strong-arm tactics were excessive and inappropriate. But to my amazement, the Chief Financial Officer acquiesced saying that he would release our receivables immediately.

"I want to hear you give that order to accounting now!" persisted Kowall.

I was stunned at our positive outcome when we finally left the building and I took a very proud Herr Kowall to one of the best restaurant in Cologne which was located near the university and, after lunch, a VIP tour of the hospital. Following his usual Schnapps and a bottle of wine he explained to me that "people like that" only respond to "harsh authority" and that he understood that there was nothing to lose in being aggressive. Shortly after the meeting began, he sensed our host both respected his experience and the justification of the threat. As we parted, I assured Kowall that his bill would be immediately paid from the company's Paris account and not placed on a long list of aging payables in Washington.

The last I saw of Kowall, he was limping from our taxicab into the train station. I watched him pass into obscurity with both a deep feeling of satisfaction and admiration. I returned to the Dom Hotel, asked the concierge to get me on the very next flight to Paris and went upstairs to pack my few belongings.

Around 5 PM, I checked into the Lufthansa lounge prior to boarding my flight. Shortly thereafter, I went through passport control and boarded the plane looking forward to the short flight and being back in Paris and catching up with our weekend plans which included activities with Homer Deberry's family.

Perhaps because I was always begging for money, I felt a sense of tense aggression in Germany which instantly disappeared once I arrived in England, Switzerland or France. While helpful flight attendants were offering pre-departure drinks and I began to unwind, a

159

green uniformed police officer entered the plane and whispered something into the purser's ear, who promptly pointed at me.

"Herr Zilvine?" the very Aryan looking officer barked. "Kommen Sie mit mir! (Come with me) Gather your things!" Rather red faced, I grabbed my carry-on luggage and followed the man out of the plane. I was taken into a room full of several customs officers, other policemen and told to wait. Within a few minutes a well dressed gentleman arrived carrying a pad and a pen.

"You know why you are being detained?" he began.

"No, sir, I have no idea. And my flight is scheduled to leave momentarily. Can we please expedite the discussion so I can get on with my trip," I said pleading.

"That will not be possible," he said emphatically. "You are on a list that forbids you to leave Germany and you are in violation of immigration laws since you have tried to escape."

"Escape?" I asked both frightened and amazed.

"Yavohl!" he said.

Suddenly I made the connection between the predicament in which I found myself and the value added tax matter.

"Does this concern my company's tax problems?" I inquired.

"The order comes from the finance ministry. You will have to answer to them," said my inquisitor.

"There is a serious misunderstanding," I began in an attempt to clarify the error. "We were advised of a minor and ongoing tax issue but I was never told that I could not leave Germany. Most importantly, I hired a well respected accountant who, in my presence, cleared the matter up with the city officials just today. You can check this with both Cologne's Chief Financial Officer and Herr Kowall," I said fumbling around to find phone numbers.

"That is not any of my concern," said the officer. "You will be detained in a city jail overnight and can have a hearing in the morning."

Terror raced through my mind as my body became tense. While I had had my share of usual problems during my adolescence, I had never been arrested or even spoken to a police officer for any offense greater than a 'fender bender.' I had visions of disappearing in some filthy, overcrowded cell with my wife and friends spending weeks trying to locate me like we had seen in the movies.

"Surely, I am allowed to make a phone call," I said in the calmest voice I could summon.

"Nur eine aber macht schnell," (only one and hurry up) said the officer becoming less patient and pointing to a phone on a table nearby.

Luckily, Perry was at home and he answered.

"Perry, I am in a terrible jam here in Cologne," I tried to explain without bursting into tears. "The immigration police will not let me leave Germany and they claim that I will have to go to jail!"

Perry knew the reason for my hurried trip to Germany as well as the ongoing financial disasters which had come to characterize the Rosemort Group with all our clients. For some unexplainable reason, it appeared to amuse Perry rather than aggravate him. I even thought I heard him stifle a laugh and he asked to speak with whoever was confronting me. I held out the phone and said that a senior diplomat

Noblesse Oblige

at the American embassy in Paris would like to speak with him. All I received was a negative nod.

"I'm afraid he will not speak with you, Perry. They are not exactly the most accommodating gang. Can you please help me?" I begged.

"Of course I can," said my friend and mentor. "But I am not sure I can be of any assistance tonight. I will call my counterpart at the embassy in Bonn and ask them to jump right on it. I'm sure if they keep you overnight you won't be treated like a common criminal," he concluded trying in vain to put my mind at rest.

"Please call Deloris and Bob Drake and, *PLEASE*, do whatever you can to help me. I am scared to death."

When I hung up, I asked if I could call Herr Kowall and have him explain the misunderstanding.

"Nur eine" (only one) was the last I heard as the detective rose and left the room.

I was placed in the back seat of a police car and taken to Cologne. As we passed the Rhine River, I could see the Dom cathedral in the distance and wondered if my days of playing an active role in the city's current history were over. Soon we reached a stark looking, concrete building where I was processed by several uniformed police officers and led to a private cell. I emptied my pockets, left my travel bag and, still wearing my business suit, and was escorted into a small but private room. It looked more like a monastery's room than a prison cell but, nevertheless, had the toilet commode against the wall of the small space. The clanking noise of the guard turning the lock will be forever impressed in my mind as forcefully as the sound of an automobile accident or a tornado.

162

A polite policeman came by shortly thereafter with a tray containing a light brown sausage, a small tube of mustard and a large piece of bread and cheese. While my initial reaction was to refuse it, I understood that would be totally self-defeating as I was both hungry and tired. So I placed my jacket and tie on the only chair, ate the 'wurst,' sat alone on my cot wondering what the following day would bring and, eventually, lay down. As I fell asleep, my only thought and hope were of Perry's words, "I will call my counterpart at the embassy in Bonn."

Like in a hospital, one does not sleep much in a jail. Noises meld with fears and each sound or clamor causes alarm. But night turned to day and by late morning the noises were reassuring. A young, professional woman arrived from the embassy in Bonn and stood by smiling while I was released and given my belongings including my passport that had never looked so good.

"It has been straightened out Mr. Silvin," she said after explaining that she was the assistant economic attaché at the embassy. "Ambassador Hillenbrand himself spoke with the authorities at the Ministry of Finance as well as German customs. Since you were not charged with a crime, you will not have a criminal record. I have a car and will take you wherever you like."

"The airport will be just fine," I said happily. "But I would be very grateful if you would accompany me to the door of the plane."

After Martin Hillenbrand retired from his long and distinguished diplomatic career he became the Director General of the Atlantic Institute for International Affairs in Paris, France where he used medical services at The International Hospital. Friends related how the former ambassador recalled the "unfortunate experience the interim administrator" had and how, as ambassador to Germany, he had been happy to find a quick solution to a frequently encountered "tax problem."

It was raining as my Air France flight took off from the "Koln-Bonn airport" but both literally and figuratively, the sun was shining in late afternoon when we landed at Orly airport in Paris. I still shudder when I hear "steuer" the German word for tax.

One very good result of the whole "Cologne affair" was the deeper relationship it created between Perry and me. I realized that I had taken a huge gamble in asking a client to intercede and help me extricate myself from a serious problem. I did not even understand the huge risk I inadvertently took. In hindsight, Perry may well have said that it was my problem and that the Rosemort Group's financial crises were interfering with our duties, to say nothing of affecting him. Instead, the 'reaching out' helped to strengthen a bond between friends, which was to last for several decades.

Chapter 4

THE AMERICAN HOSPITAL
OF POLAND

Shortly after my "contretemps" in Cologne, I received a call from Arturo Costantino, the head of American Schools and Hospitals Abroad at The State Department. Fortunately, like Perry, Arturo had come to trust me and called with some frequency to monitor our progress in both the management and the redesign of the International Hospital. Unlike "The Chairman's" visits, Arturo's were always a delight and very helpful to our team.

"We are considering using some Polish Zlotys to fund an expansion of our hospital in Poland," he explained. "I'd like you to find time to pop over to Krakow and look into how things are being done there. Then give me your reaction. I have heard positive things about the people in charge. Can you do that in a week?"

"I can get you a quick, unofficial first impression in a week, but not a management study that will look anything like we are undertaking here in Paris."

"That's exactly what I want, just your gut feelings. Project Hope is also considering responding positively to their request to fund some educational programs and I'd really like to know if they appear to be up to the challenge. Just tell me what you think after a few days with them. I'll inform their administrator and medical director so they will accommodate you."

Subjects such as "research and education" were certainly not on the radar at The International Hospital of Paris. The focus was solely on issues that related directly and indirectly to the medical staff's inflated self-opinion and financial gain. There was no discussion of medical instruction or research projects. I rather unwisely assumed that an "American Hospital" in an East European country would be equally corrupt and self- serving.

The well-respected facility was changing both its mission as well as its name from "The American Hospital" to "The Polish-American Children's Research Hospital." The change underscored a transformation of its identity and the institution's need to focus on important, unmet local medical issues. The proposed new Polish-American Hospital would, hopefully, also become a leading specialty, research facility. The hospital was located in the culturally rich town of Krakow which had served as Poland's capital for centuries before Warsaw became the main city in 1593. After the Congress of Vienna, in 1815, which redefined some of Europe's borders, Warsaw also became the "Center of the Polish Kingdom."

Both Krakow and Warsaw were leaders in urban development before the Second World War and after Poland was re-created by the Treaty of Versailles and the embedded League of Nations. Their achievements included some of the first, citywide water and sewer systems, an efficient public tram transportation network and gas works including well-lit streets. While Warsaw was devastated by the Second World War, Krakow retained many of its original buildings and architectural charm. As a result, Krakow is a beautiful, medium sized city which also has many handsome buildings with long histories including the gothic cathedral of Saint Mary's Basilica.

The only "touristy" experience I had time to undertake, while in Krakow, was to visit the once separate Jewish city of Kazimierz. The city had been the seat of Jewish culture for over five hundred years and was just now being re-discovered as an area rich in ethnic traditions and history. It became famous twenty-five years later when Stephen Spielberg made his movie *Schindler's List* in part based there. I was delighted to find charming old streets, now lined with art galleries, sidewalk cafes and smoke filed indoor restaurants. Kazimierez gave the entire city an interesting timeless feeling of history merging with modern trends and fashions. The local salt mines, later listed by UNESCO as a world monument in 1978, are a fascinating accident of nature that may date back fifteen million years. While I had hoped to go to nearby Auschwitz, my schedule did not allow any time for an excursion.

Any concerns that I may have had about encountering even a vague resemblance of resistance and suspicion similar to the International Hospital of Paris were immediately defused upon my arrival. Vasili Agnon, the hospital's executive director, and Nicholaus Gibili, the medical director, were open to questioning and visibly proud to explain both their impressive accomplishments and their ambitious goals. My first day of meetings with them was partially interrupted by the visit of a famous native Pole, Andrew Schally.

Like many other well educated people, Doctor Schally had fled Poland prior to the war and become a highly respected American physician and educator. His expertise was clearly being appreciated and absorbed by everyone on the medical staff who hung on his every word. At the time, he was a senior Medical Investigator for the Veteran's Administration. However, four years later, in 1977, Doctor Schally won the Nobel Prize in Medicine. He shared the honor with Doctor Roger Guillemin from the Salk Institute in San Diego, California for their work in peptide hormone production in the brain.

The two officers of the hospital, Gibili and Agnon, were eager to explain what they wanted to achieve and to request as much assistance from USAID as possible. Their impressive wish list centered on educational programs which, in their opinion, required the construction of a medical research facility and 240 new hospital beds. Having fresh in my mind the insistence on archaic design concepts proposed by the Chief of Staff in Paris, I tested the waters by asking Doctor Gibili how he envisioned the design of the proposed buildings.

"I can tell you the functions we hope to carry out," he answered. "But we want your input to get us professional space planners and equipment experts to recommend what we specifically require."

When asked what new medical programs the staff expected from these investments, I was equally impressed with the logical and ambitious responses, "We definitely want to expand our new cardio-vascular surgical team to address the region's pediatric congenital defects. We will want an up-to-date neonatal intensive care unit and modern surgical facilities to assure the highest level of sterility. To this end we have opened discussions with our colleagues at Harvard who work at Children's Hospital in Boston as well as other leaders in the field in Philadelphia."

The contrast to the lack of medical and intellectual curiosity I was trying to address in Paris was blatant and most informative. In Paris, any suggestion of even basic sterile techniques was viewed as a threat. Obviously, larger goals of medical research and education were never even mentioned. "Education and research" means students and students mean questions – many very intelligent and probative questions. The Polish medical staff seemed to welcome such scrutiny while the Parisian team was defensive in the extreme and vocally over-concerned with their earning potential versus higher values such as providing an improved quality of service and filling local needs.

When the two professionals asked if I could arrange for them to visit their counterparts in Paris so that they "could learn from them," I had to control both my laughter and the wording of my response. "I think what you are getting from Doctor Schally and your contacts in Boston and Philadelphia would be hard to beat," I responded as diplomatically as possible.

"Will you send us experts with the latest information?" was a typical question regardless of the subjects we were discussing. The staff simply could not obtain enough knowledge. We spent ten hours a day together, breaking only for meals, where the questions and thirst for data and assistance resumed. In my hotel room each night, I scribbled notes and, later traveling back to France, wrote a report to USAID which, I hoped would lead to the successful grants that the hospital eventually did receive. I deliberately mentioned that no physician or management representative had once discussed the issue of their personal compensation or required elements to establish their relative status. The only reference to The International Hospital of Paris in my summary report was the obvious omission of such issues in my meetings in Krakow. Subjects that were of paramount importance to Cheek and his associates in Paris were admirably, not of primary concern in Poland.

On my last night there, some ten physicians accompanied me to a historic hunting lodge where we ate venison and developed a camaraderie that was totally absent with the mercenary French and American physicians in Paris. When hard work was over, these well-rounded people also clearly played as hard as they had labored.

After such a fascinating experience with dedicated professionals, I had a renewed commitment to do the "right thing" and not be intimidated by incompetence at the political "shark tank" in Paris. How I could continue to sway the most influential of the Board members was still unclear but I knew it had to be done. One vehicle to modernize the thinking was the creation of the French Advisory Committee.

Part Four

"L'AFFAIR DEBERRY"

(THE DEBERRY FILE)

1974

&

THE WINDSORS IN THE 1950'S

AND 1960'S

Chapter 1

WEEKEND HISTORY LESSONS

Some of our other French hospital design responsibilities were working with Homer Deberry's family to site plan and prepare initial drawings for their proposed, private hospital. The Mayor's daughter, Dominique, and her charming well-groomed physician husband, Michel, had become friends. Michel liked the odd mix of social and business activities that I was becoming accustomed to at the International Hospital. I understood this as the way high level French preferred to conduct complicated business transactions. Several times a week, Michel would meet with Chris and me. We were accompanied by several other young, well-qualified physicians who Michel wanted to attract in the early planning stages of the hospital. The hope was that these colleagues of his would become primarily associated with the new hospital upon its completion.

The contract that I signed between the Rosemort Group and Michel was to be implemented in various phases with associated fees paid upon completion of each segment of our work. I knew of many private hospital projects which had been abandoned during the planning stage when the owners suddenly became aware of seemingly insurmountable obstacles. The most common of these problems were of lesser concern to us given the facts that Michel had secured preliminary financing for the hospital and the permits required to build such a facility would certainly be accelerated given his farther-in-law's influential position. Nevertheless, our attorneys advised us to have a minimum fee assigned to each phase of our design work to be due in the event the project was abandoned. During negotiations and a ceremonious signing of the contract, the minimum fee clause was not an issue of debate or apparent concern.

The site which Homer Deberry, Michel's father-in-law, had allocated for the ambitious project was well located in a high-end residential area of Neuilly. However, it was very small for the number of beds and the desired medical and surgical departments they wanted to provide. Consequently, Chris spent a significant amount of time working on the first "schematic drawings" with a clearly dedicated Michel who was conscientious in his attention to detail. We joked that we believed he spent more time in our office at the International Hospital than in his own private medical practice. There appeared to be no doubt about his, and the family's, commitment to see the project through to completion.

Michel and Dominique appreciated and shared our love for French history. We indulged that curiosity by scheduling our working weekends near the famous Chateaux of many of France's kings and queens so we could humorously and vividly recount details of French history that took place in these splendid castles.

Our favorite venue for these weekends was near the city of Amboise, at a hotel close to the Chateau de Chenonceau, arguably the most romantic and breathtaking castle of the Loire valley. The hotel we used had been a private castle and each evening during the winter months we gathered together near roaring fires in the hotel's living room. Michel would always bring Chris' drawings and the written descriptions that Bob and I prepared. He would begin his questions and I would do my best to both address his concerns and make lists for Chris to incorporate specific details the following week. In these charming locales, he asked many questions and requested changes. As a result these weekends were both fun-filled and true working holidays.

During the days, we would visit the chateau whose origins date back to the early fifteenth century with the construction of a first section which is reached at the end of a wide avenue lined with Plain trees. A series of great women were responsible for the remarkable and quixotic second and third sections of the royal estate. Diane de Poitiers, reputedly the most beautiful woman in the world, was given the responsibility to oversee the construction of the central part of the castle and its gardens by her lover, King Henri the Second. During twelve years, in the middle of the sixteenth century, Diane managed to create one of the finest examples of Renaissance architecture and formal gardens. Later, a long reception room was built onto the castle spanning the river Cher with its grand archways. The reflection of the castle on the river created an atmosphere conducive to fantasizing about the history which took place in both the gardens and inside the great chateau.

Given the castle's location along a river, Diane used clever techniques to irrigate her gardens and to create the world's first bathrooms with basins and bathtubs. Bathing was just being introduced to the previous antiquated medieval habits and it is said that the King did not like Diane to smell clean. When he was about to visit her at Chenonceau, historians allege that Henri would send a scout to her with a letter which read:

"My dear Dianne, I will be there in several days. Please stop this modern custom of bathing!"

Diane's ambitious project became the site for many loving, albeit likely odorous, meetings with the King. Their visits lasted until 1559 when Henri was fatally wounded by a lance which pierced his head armor. The accident was predicted by Nostradamus which caused him to become known as the greatest person to foresee history.

After Henri's death, his wife, Catherine de Medici, immediately ordered Diane to leave Chenonceau but allowed her to use a much less glamorous and modern castle in Chaumont.

During our several visits to Cheneonceau, we witnessed the bi-annual planting of some 40,000 flowers throughout the two main gardens which bear the names of the famous women who created them: Diane and Catherine. We marveled at how lucky we were that the estate had been spared by the destructive forces of the French Revolution in the late eighteenth century so that its beautiful Renaissance furniture and unique tapestries and paintings were preserved. In 1913 the Marques family, famed chocolatiers, bought the castle and turned it into a hospital during the ensuing years of the First World War.

Before returning to Paris we wanted to visit the magnificent, smaller and less well known Chateau de Vaux-le-Vicomte. It was of particular interest to us because the owner, the Fifth Duke of Praslin brutally murdered his wife in the castle in 1847. After she threatened to divorce him, he cut her throat and finished her off by beating her to death with a pistol. Then, the Duke's plan was to marry his mistress. However, the evidence implicating him in his wife's murder was undisputable. The young girlfriend fled to the United States and later married an Episcopal minister who would become editor of the *New York Evangelist*. The slain Duchess' son became the Sixth Duke of Praslin and would replenish the family coffers in 1874 by marrying the American heiress, Marie Elizabeth Forbes.

Meanwhile, our bills were being paid as the Deberry project development progressed and our foursome became well known at local restaurants and events. It appeared that we had begun an inseparable, long lasting relationship. This would soon end when Michel asked us to spend a weekend at Chambord.

Initially, Delores and I were not concerned when Dominique suggested we go to Chambord in separate cars and that they only join us on Saturday. The procedure had happened before when either Michel or I were delayed until Saturday. Our excitement at carrying out the plan to visit the largest of all French castles overshadowed any concerns I might have had.

Chambord was built as a massive hunting lodge by King Francis the First (Henri's father). We were thrilled to visit this other famous example of Renaissance architecture with classic Italian structures including eleven different designs of towers and eighty-four staircases. The most famous is the open, double helix staircase reputedly designed by Michelangelo so that a royal could send a mistress down the same stairs that his wife might use to ascend toward the royal suite, without either party ever seeing the other. Diane de Poitiers, it is rumored, may have been mistress to both kings: father and son.

On Saturday we toured the massive structure which Francis only used for brief hunting trips amounting to a total of seven weeks. We marveled at the almost empty four hundred and forty rooms which had been set up as the world's first apartment building because each royal guest brought most of their belongings to the hunting party. Thus the usually deserted castle was besieged by some two thousand servants who catered for their royal masters while they hunted on the thirteen thousand acre, wall enclosed property.

That evening Michel asked if he and I could have a private discussion. We sat alone in a bar as he began:

"You know, I just think that the project has become too ambitious for me to undertake at this time," he said.

"That's surprising," I answered trying to figure out what might have caused such an abrupt and complete change of direction. "The feasibility study clearly shows a need for a private hospital in that part of Paris and conservatively predicts an almost immediate profit."

"Well, my father-in-law feels it is not appropriate right now, given some political issues and we would like to place the entire deal in abeyance. There are no hard feelings, right?"

"None at all," I responded. "There will be a final billing and we will cease all work pending your decisions."

"We were hoping that you could just forgive the bill," he said to my surprise.

"But Michel, we have to bill for work done in accordance with our contract," I said becoming alarmed at his lack of business sophistication.

"We'll talk about this in Paris," he concluded rather ominously. Atypically, they left the hotel to return to Paris the same evening.

From that point on, both Michel and Dominique were "unavailable" to us. Eventually, I had to write him a letter which included Rosemort's bill. When no answer was received, and after several repeat invoices, we decided to ask our attorney to contact him. What followed next was a scene right out of the American movie, *The Godfather*.

Château de Chenonceau, France

Château de Chambord, France

Chapter 2

THE THREAT

One evening while walking back to our rented apartment from the International Hospital, I noticed to my concern that a "Denver boot" had been placed on the front wheel of my car. These devices were used in Paris to prevent a driver from moving a vehicle before paying any parking tickets or other penalties. Given that my car was parked in an assigned space for the apartment this was both odd and alarming.

Within minutes of my going upstairs the doorbell rang and I buzzed in someone who announced: "Police! Open up." I looked down the stairs as I saw two all leather clad police officers climbing the stairs.

"The Mayor wants to see you," one said. "Follow us."

I quickly told Delores what was occurring and went downstairs with my escorts to a waiting police car parked on the sidewalk in front of the building. A few neighbors watched with very curious looks as we drove off to the town hall.

The magnificent building sitting amid formal gardens is located on what is now called Avenue Achille Peretti. It is built in traditional Louis-Napoleon, "empire style" with two square towers and a central area made up of three archways on the ground floor. The police officers escorted me through these arches into a large foyer where

Deberry's secretary, the father of France's current President and head of the UMP Party, Nicholas Sarkozy, was waiting for me.

"His Excellency wants to see you," said the senior Monsieur Sarkozy. "You will follow me."

We ascended the wide stone staircase, past several secretaries' desks and reached a tall set of gold gild doors. An aide knocked at the door before opening and ushering me in. Monsieur Sarkozy left me at the door as the Mayor rose from behind a beautiful Empire style desk at the far end of the room at least fifty feet away.

"My dear René!" exclaimed the Mayor and President of the French Senate, his arms extended foreword to embrace me. "What a great pleasure to see you again. Please let us sit over here and chat." The friendly charm was both surprising and, under the circumstances, a bit frightening.

Deberry motioned me to a sitting area off to the left of his desk and began:

"I understand that you, my daughter and Michel have enjoyed numerous weekends while studying French history."

"Oui, Monsieur le Maire," (Yes Mister Mayor) I responded.

"I also understand that the four of you are enjoying many evenings at some of *my* city's best restaurants and clubs."

The words "my city" were emphasized.

"Oui, Monsieur le Maire."

"Dominique also tells me that she has grown so very comfortable traveling with you."

"Thank you, Monsieur le Maire."

"I have also followed the very ambitious plans that Michel has been working on with you for his dream of a hospital."

"Yes, we have sir," I answered. "In fact we have progressed quite far in the work…"

"You know, René, you are a young man and I hope you will not be offend if I give you some fatherly advice. I am a Corsican. Do you know what the characteristics of a Corsican are?" he asked.

My blank, rather frightened stare was answer enough.

"We are well known," he continued, "for our loyalty to friends and for our fierce fights with our enemies. These fights make Sicilian vendettas look like child's play."

I took a deep breath before he continued.

"We do enormous favors for our friends and we are prepared to fight to the death against our enemies. Now it seems that you have offended me in several ways."

"How did I offend you, Monsieur le Maire?" I asked.

"Well, for openers you live in my city without proper permits."

"But, I was told…."

The mayor cut me off and continued, "Regardless of what you may have heard, you are working in my city, at the International Hospital, which is your company's largest client. You are doing this without proper residency or work permits. I am also curious to note that your car has an American license plate. Now you know that, eventually, the drawings you are preparing for the replacement hospital will come on that desk right over there," he pointed at his desk. "For my approval. There are always many grey areas in the design of a major institution in a well-regulated and historic city such as *mine*. As a Corsican, I would be very willing to lean in directions which will allow your company to appear as heroes of design innovation. And, it goes without saying that your infractions of being here illegally could be considered details which are easily remedied. As your enemy on the other hand, I could create endless delays for the hospital and see that you are charged for being here without papers. I could make it apparent that I am not in favor of anything you propose for the hospital."

I sat there completely breathless and dumbfounded.

"Finally, you must understand that my son-in-law, Michel, is idealistic. One day, I am sure he will own a lovely and modern hospital. For now however, I have deemed his plan as just that, a plan of a dreamer."

"But we have undertaken a significant amount of work," I began, "and prepared numerous design plans which…"

"Yes, yes," continued the Mayor. "We will have to abandon this effort. Now there is a matter of one remaining detail," he said as he rose and walked over to his desk where he picked up a file. "You are billing Michel for work on a project that will never be built. That is not reasonable."

"But there is a specific clause in our contract that states…."

"Perhaps I have not made myself perfectly clear," he interrupted yet again. "As Mayor, I can guarantee the successful implementation of your biggest project or I can make sure that you are persecuted for an illegal presence here and block your company's huge French project. As your friend, I'd like to receive you at our summer home in Corsica but as your enemy I will never see you again and I can cause… let's call them serious inconveniences for you. Now Dominique is waiting in a living room on this floor and hopes to have a glass of champagne with you. Would you like that or would you rather leave here as my enemy?"

"I think I have understood very clearly, Monsieur le Maire. I'd love to see Dominique again."

"Wonderful," he exclaimed and embraced me. "One last thing, Jean-Jacques Guerlain has told me that you plan to create a French advisory committee to assist the International Hospital. If we are friends, I will agree to serve on this committee. I think it would be extremely helpful for you if I, as both Mayor of the city and President of the French Senate were by your side to assist you. So, you may add my name to your list. Now, go have that drink and enjoy another weekend in our countryside while you study French history. In fact, I understand you wanted to see the chateau of Chaumont where Diane de Poitiers went after being exiled from the beautiful Chenonceau by HER enemy, Catherine de Medici – also an Italian who understood the differences between friends and enemies."

My knees were wobbly. But that was a feeling I knew I preferred to have them broken. I walked through a different set of double doors to be greeted by Dominique who looked as beautiful and sexy as always. Neither of us discussed Michel, the project or the meeting I had just finished with her father. We drank several glasses of champagne and made plans to meet the following weekend.

Chapter 3

CHAUMONT

The following weekend, we four friends met in Chaumont as if nothing had happened. We did not discuss the hospital and Michel did not bring any architectural plans or work. It was as if there never had been a contract or a plan to build a hospital for the family. We visited the Chateau with the same avid curiosity for its history but there was a clear strain in the way we interacted. The "touchy-feely" French way among close friends was definitely absent.

The Chateau itself was originally built in the tenth century as a fortress. Therefore it looked like a fort and not a luxury castle like Chenonceau. Catherine de Medici bought it the year her husband, King Henri the Second, died. Her initial intent was to use the chateau to house Nostradamus and follow his subsequent predictions about what was in store for her, the royal children and France in general. But The Queen soon decided to shift these and other activities to the much more comfortable and modern Chateau de Chenonceau; she forced Diane de Poitiers to swap castles.

The Chateau de Chaumont was of additional interest to us as it was bought in 1750 by Jacques-Donatien Le Ray who was considered by some as the "father of the American Revolution." A great admirer of the new world and supporter of the American War of Independence, Le Ray frequently entertained the visiting Benjamin Franklin in the castle. Dominique's father had once again arranged for us to have a private tour of the castle and to enter closed – or roped off – areas. The chateau's curator asked us to sit on the very furniture where Benjamin Franklin is said to have laid out his plans and requests for funds to support the American war effort across the Atlantic. Afterwards the head gardener escorted us through the English style gardens which were closed to the public as they were being readied for the great annual garden festival.

On Sunday, we left Chaumont early so that Delores could drop me off at the newly opened Charles de Gaulle International airport to catch a flight to Washington, DC. I had decided that I must deliver the bad financial news to my father-in-law and our finance director in person. I knew that a difficult discussion would ensue, so it appeared essential to conduct it in person and not over the phone.

Sitting with me in the first class section of the TWA 747 was Betty Riddle. Her husband, The Very Reverend Sturgis L. Riddle was the dean of the American Episcopal Cathedral of Paris. The couple filled a highly visible and social position in the Franco-American community in France. As such, there was considerable overlap of influential officers, deacons and board members of the hospital, the embassy and the cathedral. Dean Riddle had been an inactive member of the International Hospital's Board of Governors for ten years. I was very impressed that he was considered among the twenty-five most influential people in the 1960's civil rights movement.

Perry had brought me to numerous private meetings with Dean Riddle to lobby our case for improved management techniques at the hospital and to obtain the Dean's vote of confidence when he certainly would be approached by the American physicians. Dean

Riddle was a kind, somewhat rotund, yet tall and imposing man who preferred to remain above such discussions and battles. In fact, he rarely attended the hospital's board meetings. Nevertheless, it was important for us to have him aware of our position and the trouble that it had generated. Perhaps as a "concession" for his taciturn support, Dean Riddle asked me to read from the Gospel at several Sunday services.

When we left the rectory, the day the Dean had made his request of me; I turned to Perry in the back of an Embassy car and said:

"Perry, I was a bit taken aback that you agreed for me that I would read from the Gospel in front of the congregation for the next several Sundays. As you know, I have no religious instruction and do not practice – or believe in – structured religion."

"That's irrelevant," said the diplomat Perry. "You need to be as visible as possible in the American community in Paris and there is no better way to achieve this than to accept Riddle's offer. Just pretend to be pious and 'make nice' in the rectory after Mass." As a result of these "readings" and my meetings with the Riddles at the Cathedral I had become quite friendly with, and fond of, them both. When Perry heard that I was returning to Washington for a few days he arranged for me to fly with Mrs. Riddle who coincidentally was also returning to the capital for a medical reasons. I found it both interesting and wise that Mrs. Riddle would not be treated at the International Hospital.

"You must sit next to her and have someone in DC accompany her to the doctors and hospitals," said Perry.

"Of course, Perry," I said. "We'll put a car and driver at her disposal and do our best to assist her in any way possible."

Mrs. Riddle was going to be staying at the Deanery of the Washington National Cathedral on Mount Saint Alban in Washington, DC with our mutual friends Frank and Harriet Sayre. Frank Sayre was both Dean of the Washington Cathedral and a board member of the Rosemort Group. Everyone had many things in common and was comfortable with each other. As President Woodrow Wilson's grandson, Dean Sayre was an important figure in Washington in much the same religious and political way as the Riddles were in Paris.

"You will get a good laugh on the plane," said Perry.

He was referring to the fact that Mrs. Riddle's nickname was "Mrs. Malaprop" after the Richard Brinsley Sheridan's character in his famous play "The Rivals." Both the fictional character and Mrs. Riddle were capable of enunciating the most amazing malapropisms. A malapropism is the use of similar sounding words but with totally different meanings.

As we took our seats that had been reserved next to each other, Mrs. Riddle said that she was tired because she and the Dean had hosted a dinner the previous evening for the "Lesbian Ambassador." I nearly spit out my orange juice and immediately understood that she meant "the Lebanese Ambassador." During the flight she pronounced another, unfortunately sad, one saying: "The reason I am returning to DC is that I have a megalomania on my leg." Again, I knew that she meant "a melanoma," a cancerous tumor.

The trip was largely uneventful as the lovely Mrs. Riddle explained that, after twenty-five years as Dean of The American Cathedral; they were retiring that October and moving to New York where the Dean had been appointed Honorary Minister of Saint Bartholomew's Church as well as a Trustee of the Board of Foreign Parishes. She reminisced about their early posts in Europe, shortly after the war, serving in Florence, Italy before moving to the prestigious position in Paris. She described all of Dean Riddle's awards including the one that impressed me the most: Chevalier of the "Legion d'Honneur," France's most revered decoration. The charming slightly bucked teeth but stately lady spoke of many achievements and milestones in their lives as if in anticipation of her pending demise. She described the three books the Dean wrote: *One Hundred Years* (1950), *We Believe in Prayer* (1958) and *That Day with God* (1965). Mrs. Riddle passed away within two years of our flight and all of Dean Riddle's papers "ascended" to the collection of historical documents in the official archives of the Episcopal Church in 2005.

Chateau de Chaumont, France

Chapter 4

WASHINGTON DC

I was at the Rosemort office early the following day, well before Martin arrived. I used the occasion to speak to the few, loyal remaining consultants. The reports I got underscored the disastrous financial shape as well as the general overall morale of the company.

One topic of discussion was the only prospective new project for the company. The University of Guadalajara in Mexico had issued an "RFP" (request for proposals) from hospital management companies to undertake an effort rather similar to the scope of our mission in Paris. Specifically, it involved the preparations of a master plan for the reconstruction of the large university hospital with a focus on managing the new facility. The consultants I spoke with had accompanied Martin to Mexico to make the presentation.

"How is it going in Guadalajara?" I asked.

"The problem," answered the consultant, "is that the selection committee is correctly focused on management of the project and mostly on running the hospital."

"That's great," I answered. "The real money for us is in the fees paid for management services."

"Yes," he proceeded. "I hope you will not take this in the wrong way, but we could not get Martin to respond to any of their concerns and questions about *management*. He only wanted to address his design concepts. I could see that while they were initially impressed with our credentials, we began to lose their attention when Martin did not describe how we proposed to *run* the facility. This could be a great job but we have to be more responsive to their requirements."

With the discussion over, I proceeded to another office to face the main issue I had come to Washington to argue.

Lee Willis, our Chief Financial Officer, had followed the alarming evolution of the rapidly declining "quality" of the Deberry receivable. We had collected approximately $50,000 on the project and were owed another $80,000. Such a sum usually meant the difference between being able to meet the company's payroll and keeping the long list of creditors at bay or slipping further behind in both areas.

When Martin arrived, he, Lee and I sat together in his office. I described the "conversation" I had with Deberry, as well as his huge influence and importance in French politics in general and specifically in the city of Neuilly where the International Hospital was located.

Martin and Lee were very concerned. They had come to expect the large sums of money that the three European projects were repatriating. They even took the transfers for granted, without much regard to the difficulties of obtaining immediate and often early payments. Martin began his usual behavior when he felt threatened; he turned his desk chair toward the wall, his back to Lee and me, and began chewing on his tie. Lee and I poured over the short term cash flow projections and made a list of which creditors could be further delayed and which executives may be willing to forego a pay check. Unfortunately, since Martin's personal financial situation was as critical as the company's, he was always unwilling to take a pay cut much less skip

194

one pay period completely. Thus it was practically impossible to convince an executive, whether consultant or architect, to reduce their income if the company's head and proprietor did not also do so.

By late morning we decided to meet with our loan officer at Riggs National Bank which, as our bank, had extended our line of credit to the maximum and was apparently unwilling to make any more concessions. We weighed the legal cost of pursing the Deberry debt versus the potential return. When it became apparent that the consensus in the room was to pursue legal action I made my case:

"Look guys, I don't think you are getting the point. Homer Deberry is an enormously influential and powerful man. Try to draw the parallel of Deberry to Paris and Neuilly with Mayor Frank Rizzo in Philadelphia…"

"I don't understand," interrupted the banker.

"Well, Mayor Frank Rizzo in Philadelphia is known as the 'Cisco Kid' and is fearless as well as action oriented. After serving as a hard line police commissioner, he was elected Mayor six years ago. He formed his own secret police force and is responsible for widespread acts of brutality and beatings. That is the parallel with Deberry."

"OK, go on," said the banker.

"Both men are respected *and* feared. Deberry made it perfectly clear to me that if we pursue this receivable, he will torpedo us at the International Hospital. I have enough enemies on the medical staff without having a huge political fight with no ability to counter. Conversely, he was clear about granting the hospital a building permit for our project when the time comes and even serving on the French advisory board I am putting together. While it is unbelievable to think of foregoing $80,000, I would rather do that than be fired by The State Department when it is made clear to them that it is we who are hindering the replacement of the International Hospital. We, the very group hired and well paid to make it happen!"

"OK," yelled Martin, "let the French bastards keep their money. I have saved this company many times and will do so again. There is as much money in this new job in Guadalajara as in both French projects. I'll stay on it and will handle it all by myself. You'll see – we'll get the job."

Many worried faces looked at me while Martin went back to chewing his tie. Eventually it was agreed not to have the attorneys proceed with attempts to collect the money in Paris. As the meeting was breaking up, the banker beckoned me to follow him. I escorted him to the elevator where he revealed his position.

"Have you seen the profit and loss for the whole company?"

"Yes, of course, it is alarming."

"It's more than alarming," he said in a worried voice. "You need to know that regardless of the fact that you are sending back nearly three quarters of the company's operating needs from Europe the losses are escalating. There have been no new projects on this side of the Atlantic. There is no way we can extend any more credit to Martin personally or the company. Let us be very clear about that."

"What do you expect me to do?" I asked.

"Just continue the very best way you can in France and Germany with the small staff you have. But brace yourself for the day when it may be lights off here in Washington. I'd like to add something totally off the record. Do I have your word that what I am about to say will remain between us?"

"Yes, of course," I said.

"If I were you, I'd try to secure a job with the International Hospital separate from Rosemort. I just can't see them pulling the company out of the nose dive. You are young and can be ruined by a bankruptcy. You have a good relationship with this Perry Culley. God knows we wonder why he approves all your bills, but it won't last forever. I'll deny I said this if you repeat it, but you need to consider jumping ship and soon."

My return to Paris was much less enjoyable than listening to Betty Riddle on the westbound flight. I fretted myself about what Martin would do if – or rather when – the company was shut down and he had zero revenue and huge liabilities. I decided that I'd have to focus on doing the best possible job but to have a heart to heart discussion with Delores about the likely plight facing her parents.

But fortunately, I had something much more enjoyable to look forward to: the Duchess had asked me to accompany her to a Christmas party at Maxim's given by the twenty-four year old Christina Onassis, daughter of famed billionaire Aristotle Onassis and step-daughter of Jacqueline Kennedy Onassis.

Chapter 5

MAXIM'S EVENT

As usual, I met Wallis at Le Bois in order to escort her to dinner. When I arrived, one butler dressed in black tails and two footmen, in red jackets; stood erect as yet another footman opened the carved metal double doors. The butler showed me into the main living room. Once again, I noticed how the beautiful nineteenth century home was cozy, if a bit cluttered. Wallis had referred to it as a "miniature palace" and, thanks to her tireless ingenuity, it certainly was.

It gave visitors an immediate sensation of being both grand and warm. It was inviting unlike a palace or castle. "Le Bois" or "The Woods" sits in the middle of a large garden with mature trees in the Bois de Boulogne, Paris' beautiful park on the edge of the city. Amazing one-of-a-kind antiques filled the home to capacity and memorabilia of the Duke's brief tenure as King of England could be seen everywhere: a beautiful collection of Royal silver and gold boxes and his abdication document were on display. Equally prominent were pictures, sculptures and mementoes of the couple's many adored pug dogs.

"'Her Royal Highness' will be down presently," said the butler. "May I fix you a drink?"

With a drink in hand, I walked around the crowded main drawing room. The walls were silver blue and the furniture was all Louis XV with ornate upholstery. On one delicate table stood two gold candlesticks framing a black and white picture of Edward in his investiture robes when he became Prince of Wales. His handsome face seemed a bit sad and his eyes looked tired for such a young man. There were candlesticks everywhere as well as a candle-lit Baccarat chandelier. This room was more formal than the others and contained fewer memorabilia: only one porcelain Pug and a few famous pictures but no family portraits. It was different from the rooms which contained more Royal memorabilia, pictures of Edward and his mother, Queen Mary. Conspicuously absent in any room were pictures or paintings of Edward's father, King George V. This central living room was ceremonial and bore few personal mementoes. Only one favorite picture of Wallis' was visible on a table; it was taken in an evening gown in 1945 and marked the year the New York Dress Institute put Wallis on the "best dressed list of 1945." She was named on this list many more times but cherished the first and only year when she was ranked as number 10. With her hearty laugh she would tell guests "that's the year I made it by the skin of my teeth!"

I thought of the title of de Maupassant's book, *Une Vie* (a whole life) when, on previous visits, I had studied the Duke's famous collection of silver and gold boxes in other rooms as well as the abundance of pictures of the famous trips they had made together. It was easy for me to fantasize about the many ship crossings because the Duchess and I had discussed them on several occasions. I knew I was standing in an historic home which had passed its prime. The Duke was gone and I wondered how long Wallis would be able to carry on. She was clearly showing signs of more than occasional "confusion." Their post-war history flashed through my mind. These I had to dream of as I had only read contradicting accounts about their history, heard rumors during my entire life as well as listened to accurate stories from my mother.

So many bizarre things had happened to this uncanny couple. For instance, there were the two never solved murders of friends: one in the Bahamas and the other on Long Island. Both had occurred after Wallis and the Duke had just left the victim's homes.

Wallis and Edward had kept an inchoate group of friends which, to the surprise of royal watchers, began when the Duke was King. These ranged from royalty and politicians, to socialites who invited them on some of the world's best yachts, offered the use of private railway cars and included them at all the social sports events such as polo, live pigeon shoots and horse races. There had been almost as many racy parties - some erupting in disputes amongst the guests – as there had been regal gatherings. The night Bill Woodward was killed by his wife, Ann, in Oyster Bay, Long Island in 1955, the party had broken up because of an argument. Their close and much gossiped about long term relationship with the flamboyant Woolworth heir, Jimmy Donahue, had also ended in a public display of tempers. It was said that the Duke "liked Donahue but that Wallis loved him." In one of the very few times that Wallis was away from Edward, she traveled to New York alone in order to attend several events with Jimmy. During an interview shortly thereafter, Edward R. Murow asked the Duke how he would like to spend the rest of his life. He turned toward Wallis and spontaneously said, "Together."

The late 1940's and 1950's may have been their most carefree years as they traveled back and forth between the two homes in France, the Warldorf Towers in New York and generous and admiring friends in Palm Beach. The idea of being political advisors or even holding any official position had been abandoned right after the war. Meanwhile, their role as premier socialites was solidly established. It was said, "Where the Windsors went, society followed." Perhaps because of their high visibility, many questions and rumors circulated about sexual oddities, the Duke's alleged "enslavement" by Wallis and their pre-war political allegiances.

Unfortunately in the previous decades, the Windsors had associated with many notorious and infamous people including their close friend for twenty years and host at their wedding, Charles Bedaux, as well as Wallis' early attorney, Armand Gregoire. Both men were tried as Nazi agents. Gregoire was sentenced to a life of hard labor which must have been quite a shock considering the luxuries he had become accustomed to.

In keeping with his character, Bedaux's fate was convoluted. He was first arrested by the Nazis in 1942, but released on the condition that he must maintain oversight on the construction of a Nazi oil pipeline from Algeria to Dakar using prisoners of war as slave laborers. As a guarantee that he would not flee German control, his wife, Fern, was to remain at the grand Chateau de Condé under an ultra-luxurious house arrest. While in Algeria, Bedaux was arrested by the Americans, charged with treason as an "industrial collaborator" and sent to trial in Miami. At his opening hearings, he told the court that he worked for the Nazis after they occupied France because "the Germans were the only ones left in Paris to do business with." Had his trial proceeded, Bedaux would undoubtedly have implicated many other American "industrial collaborators." But on Valentine's Day of 1943 he was found dead in his room. It was never clear if he was murdered, deliberately committed suicide or simply conveniently took an accidental overdose of sleeping pills. His widowed wife, Fern, lived out a long yet solitary life at the Chateau de Candé in France.

The list of Wallis' friends who met tragic ends grew. Count Gallazzo Ciano, the suspected father of her unborn child, but certainly her lover in China, had a controversial tenure while serving in Mussolini's government. To ingratiate himself with his father-in-law, "Il Duce" as Mussolini was called, he most likely arranged for the assassination of the Rosselli brothers in 1937. The Rosselli family was a highly respected, leading anti-fascist group who were trying to overthrow Mussolini. During Ciano's early years in the Mussolini government, he was active in the formulation of Italy's foreign policy. He was rewarded by Il Duce, as he was offered one of the highest positions in the government: that of foreign minister, when the young Count was only thirty-three.

After the allied invasion of Sicily in 1942, Ciano realized that the fascists would lose the war. He urged his father-in-law to make a "separate peace" with the allies thus breaking off relations with Hitler. Ciano was rebuked by Mussolini who made the famous statement that he would fight until the "last Italian soldier was killed." Ciano continued his efforts to convince Mussolini to surrender which led Mussolini to remove Ciano as foreign minister and gave him the relatively unimportant position as liaison officer with the Vatican. Undaunted, Ciano then tried to rally Mussolini's ministers into returning authority over the Italian military to Italy's king. Naturally, this further infuriated Mussolini who, in spite of pleas for mercy from his daughter, Edda, had his son-in-law tried for treason and, upon his conviction, had Ciano executed by firing squad in Verona in January of 1944. Along with three other convicted government officials, he was shot in the back – signifying the death of a traitor. By this time, the war was nearly over and it is believed that Mussolini had Ciano shot to convince Hitler that

Il Duce was still strong and in control of his government. Mussolini, himself, was executed a year later as he was caught near Como while he was attempting to escape to Switzerland.

It seemed that so many of the Windsors' friends and acquaintances had ruthlessly bet on both sides of the European conflict and, thus, ended their lives in tragic ways. Wallis, on the other hand, only suffered the long-term effects of rumors about her involvement with Nazi Germany. Perhaps the most convincing evidence of Hitler's affection for Wallis is the fact that all her treasured belongings, housed in her two French residences as well as in storage, amazingly survived the Nazi pillage.

Fortunately for Wallis' reputation she had hired a public relations advisor, Guido Orlando, in the early 1950's and also an attorney, Suzanne Blum. As a result the unending notorious rumors began to lessen, legal battles disappeared and more good deeds and charitable work, such as serving on the International Hospital's board, began.

Le Bois, the magnificent home in which I was standing had been leased in 1952 and symbolized the beginning of their "settling down" after wandering around the globe for the first sixteen years of their marriage. That same very eventful year, Edward's brother, King George VI, died and his young daughter became Queen Elizabeth the Second. I thought of what the Duke felt at both his mother's and his brother's funerals. Perhaps as a result of these reflections, Edward found some happy days when they purchased their first home, The Mill, outside of Paris.

As mentioned earlier, the couple had never bought properties but rather found ingenious ways to live in very grand homes for very little – or no – money. But what was known as "The Mill" did belong to them.

It was a series of unassuming stone buildings an hour from Paris. It was there that Edward returned to his love of gardening and landscaping which he practiced while he was Prince of Wales and even during the eleven months, in 1936, when he was King.

The decade of 1950 further solidified the Windsors' unequalled role of society's royals. Before the war, French aristocracy had mostly avoided the Windsors - possibly because of the "HRH issue." But things were different after the war, almost as if a new page had been turned on many issues regarding Wallis. Her role as hostess and wife extraordinaire became unquestioned.

The dinner parties were perfectly planned and executed in Wallis' inimitable, brilliant and slightly compulsive fashion. Discussing the way Wallis planned her dinner parties, gourmet food connoisseur and specialty food boutique owner, Edmund Bory said that the Duchess "was not just a perfectionist but a powerful perfectionist." Biographer Ralph Martin said that "in the Duchess' home, the crystal sparkled, the leather gleamed, the furniture shone. During a meal, her eyes worked overtime to keep the butler aware of filled ashtrays which needed to be emptied and glasses that needed refilling. She had a small gold covered book in which she wrote comments and complaints about meals and other things which she then told the butler." Indeed, her dinner parties more closely resembled a well choreographed play than a carefree party.

By the end of the decade, both Edward and Wallis had experienced their first indications of significant health problems. On occasion their drinking was excessive and the Duke was a chain smoker; these abuses and constant late night parties had begun to take their toll.

During the 1960's the couple's life continued to become more serene but was punctuated by increasing health problems. Wallis and

Edward each had several surgeries, including an abdominal aneurism repair for the Duke in Houston, Texas in late 1964. After careful analysis, the Duke selected famed Houston based surgeon, Michael DeBakey, who the Duke referred to as "the maestro" to perform the "triple A" (abdominal aortic aneurism) surgery. Following the operation, he and the Duchess flew back to New York, which was difficult for Wallis given her acute fear of flying which dated back to 1920 when she witnessed a friend who was a Navy pilot crash and die.

At least one Windsor biographer erroneously claims this Houston to New York commercial flight was the Duchess' last flight for over a decade. A recently discovered picture, however, reveals that the Duchess flew again aboard Marjorie Merryweather Post's private aircraft – most likely a DC 3 named "the Merryweather" – on April 29, 1968. The picture shows a very relaxed Duke, carrying a *New York Times*, boarding the aircraft with a worried Duchess trying her best to smile for the photographer; she was wearing a rare, above-the-knee dress, trying to conceal her hands.

If only the same diligence applied to selecting DeBakey had been repeated when the Duke first had signs of throat cancer or the Duchess underwent surgery for bleeding stomach ulcers, the royal couple's ends, especially the Duchess', may have been more humane.

Throughout the late 1950' and early 1960's Edward worked in his garden at the Mill and their parties became tame in relation to what they had been. Wallis' role as a supportive and encouraging wife was solidified and soared beyond any reasonable person's ability to criticize or accuse her of being self-centered when it came to her devotion to her husband. In May of 1968, *Woman's Wear Daily* said "the Duchess of Windsor may be the best wife in the world," a comment that most assuredly gave Wallis the confirming endorsement that she so wanted and deserved.

The previous year, 1967, saw the first of several gestures of rapprochement between Wallis and the Royal family; Edward and Wallis received a specific invitation to be present at the placement of a commemorative plaque honoring the late Queen Mary, David's mother. Although it was likely issued fearing a public outcry if the Duke were seen at the celebration alone, the move must have brought Wallis great satisfaction. The Duke was likely even more gratified by giving credence to his frequent statement that "we must never go anywhere unless we both can enter though the front door."

It was in the 1960's and early 1970's that they embarked on what so many socialites did and still do in their late sixties; they searched for the fountain of youth. Wallis had at least three partial face-lifts and they made an annual pilgrimage to Switzerland.

A Swiss physician by the name of Paul Niehans owned a small, specialty clinic above Lake Geneva near Vevey, where Charlie Chaplin lived. At "La Prairie," his clients included the Pope, Somerset Maugham, Charlie Chaplin, George Burns, Carry Grant and many of the Windsors' friends, including my parents. Niehans had developed a "cure for aging" which consisted of injecting lamb blood components, mostly a part of white blood cells called macrophages, from specific organs like the thymus and lamb fetus into his patients. While he was certainly on the right track and can arguably be called the father of modern stem cell research, his methods were primitive given today's level of science. The $15,000 "cure" lasted two weeks, during which time the patients remained in his clinic, ate his healthy food, and abandoned smoking, drinking and sleeping pills. While it is likely that the serums did neither good nor harm, most people left feeling totally rejuvenated because of the obvious detoxification they experienced during their stay. Niehans' clinic later manufactured beauty products now known under the trade name of "Clinique."

On another table at Le Bois that evening, I noticed a picture of the current Queen visiting Wallis only eighteen months earlier when she came to pay respects to her dying uncle. Most reports suggest that there never was reconciliation between the Queen, her mother and the Duke. This is not true. There was a meandering and convoluted rapprochement typical of the Royal morays and the changing values of the twentieth century. I daydreamed about Edward's death when he is alleged to have shouted "Mama" three or four times before he expired. If true, it is unclear if his last thoughts were of Wallis (who did play a maternal role in his life) or his mother, Queen Mary.

In his book *The Duchess of Windsor. The Uncommon Life of Wallis Simpson*, Greg King offers details of the Duke's final moments and of the following days. According to his account, the Duke's favorite dog, Black Diamond, was on his master's bed the night of May 27 and the early morning of May 28, 1972. The Duchess had very rarely left her ailing husband's side. Around midnight, the Duke is alleged to have opened his eyes and said to Wallis: "Darling go get some rest." The Duke passed quietly away in his sleep a few hours later at 2:20 AM on the morning of May 28. A nurse woke the Duchess who went to her still warm husband's body and is reported to have kissed him saying" My David, My David."

Later the same morning, as the news fanned out to the Parisian community, Le Bois became the scene of great activity. One of the first dignitaries to arrive was France's Foreign Minister, Maurice

Schumann, followed by Italy's exiled King Umberto and the Duchess' friend and favorite dress designer, Hubert de Givenchy. De Givenchy revealed details of his visit during an interview shortly thereafter saying, "Understandably the Duchess went to pieces." He explained that the Duchess asked him to quickly prepare an outfit for her to wear at the Royal funeral in London, which he did in record-breaking time.

Finally, my reverie was interrupted when the butler announced that "Son Altesse Royale" (Her Royal Highness) would be coming down and, through his gesturing, indicated that I should greet her at the bottom of the circular staircase.

"Do you know what I have decided, René?" asked a joyous Wallis immediately.

"No Duchess, please tell me," I answered.

"I have decided it is time to go back to the United States for a visit and I shall take your suggestion and travel on the Michelangelo or her sister ship the Rafaello," which the Duchess did accompanied by her treasured private secretary, Johanna Schutz, a maid, and two pugs in both the summers of 1974 and 1975. In Hugo Vickers book, *Behind Closed Doors, the Tragic Untold Story of the Duchess of Windsor* he writes "The Duchess stayed mainly in her cabin and her name did not appear on the passenger list. Sometimes she dined in the dining room, largely out of consideration for Miss Schutz to make the voyage more interesting for her."

The Duchess was in a good frame of mind the evening of this event and, luckily for me, was in a chatty and reminiscent mood. Her beautiful black hair was typically yet stylishly parted in the middle, this time creating two fairly large half crescents rather than her usual more severe pulled back style. She wore a formal, plain, black satin dress, diamond earrings and a diamond pin. As usual she was timelessly elegant, regal and grand. As we prepared to leave, a butler helped her into a full-length white mink coat and handed her the black purse she had chosen to use.

"The press has reported that this is my first official outing since David died," she said as we got into a black Rolls Royce. "But the press often gets it wrong. What was the gala at Longchamp supposed to be?" she asked with more than a hint of sarcasm.

The Duchess was referring to the fundraiser benefiting the International Hospital which took place six months earlier. That soiree *had* been her debut back into Parisian society.

"It did take a year after David's death for me to want to be seen in large groups like this. Incidentally, Christina said that she knew you. Where did you meet?"

"On several occasions in Switzerland, Duchess. We skied together," I replied.

"I never took to skiing," she said. "David did but then he liked so many sports. He was way ahead of his times. Let's do our best to be gay for the sake of appearances." Then using her often said line: "Remember noblesse oblige, René. The hardest thing I ever had to do was to put on a good face during David's illness when the Queen came to bid adieu to him. David was confined to his bed but he insisted on being dressed shaved and seated before the Queen entered his room. He insisted that he stand upon seeing her. She made peace with him that day which was so important."

"Did she come alone?" I asked.

"Heavens no. Prince Philip escorted her as well as my favorite, Prince Charles. It was so odd being with the current Prince of Wales. I do like Charles and he was very gracious to me that difficult day. I already felt like a widow and had begun dressing only in black and I could see Charles was pained for me. Most importantly, he stuck by my side most of the two days of the funeral in London shortly thereafter. A sensitive young man!" Prince Charles later revealed that, speaking about the Duke at his funeral, the Duchess repeated, "He gave up so much for so little."

When the Queen's plane arrived in London carrying the Duchess for the state funeral, it was the Queen's beloved uncle, and the Windsors' long-tenured friend, Lord Louis Mountbatten who met the plane. According to Greg King, Mountbatten quoted the Duchess as follows: "He was my entire life. I can't begin to think what I m going to do without him. He gave up so much for me, and now he has gone. I always hoped that I would die before him."

Shortly before the June 5, 1972 funeral, Mountbatten and Prince Charles escorted the bereaved Duchess to see the Duke's body lying in State at Saint George's Chapel at Windsor where some 60,000 people solemnly filed by to pay their last respects to their former King.

Sadly, it was during that final visit to England that Wallis had returned to and slept at, Buckingham Palace for the first time since Edward had been King. One can only imagine the Duke's joy had he known that his great wish of having Wallis received at the palace was finally granted.

During the days surrounding the funeral, some observers thought the Duchess exhibited her first signs of confusion. However, it is impossible to draw that conclusion when one considers Wallis was stressed and grieved beyond comprehension. The Windsors' thirty-six years together had brought the odd couple so tightly close to each other - their secrets securely locked up deep within their minds.

The theory that the Duchess experienced any prolonged confusion is further dispelled by the Countess Romanones who quoted Wallis' humorous remarks regarding the Queen mother's outfit as follows: It looked like "she had opened some old trunk and pulled out a few rags and draped them on herself. How David would have laughed."

The Duchess picked up the thread of our conversation: "When he died, I knew nothing would ever be the same and those fun-filled trips and events were over," she said with a sigh. "Of course I curtsied to her Majesty at David's funeral but I could not bring myself to give the Queen mother that satisfaction. I am glad to say that she noticed it of course. Some said I was confused, but I was simply making a point. I could not have been too demented to ask the Archbishop of Canterbury where my assigned grave would be!"

I had heard the famous stories. The Duchess had, in fact, refused to curtsy to her old foe, the Queen mother, who Wallis blamed for being denied the title of HRH. At the gravesite, Wallis allegedly told the archbishop that even though she was a "small woman," she could "not fit" in the allocated, relatively small spot adjacent to Edward's as the Queen had allowed. She continued by strongly recommending an adjacent hedge be "moved back" to enlarge her grave. Competent historians, including Hugo Vickers, challenge this detail of history because, in fact, there is no hedge near the side-by-side graves of the iconic couple.

Importantly, Wallis was treated perfectly at the funeral, which would most certainly have given the Duke huge satisfaction. It was almost as if his life's work was complete. Prince Charles called the Duchess "Aunt Wallis" and said he hoped he would be as good a Prince of Wales as "Uncle David." Wallis was told that she could do whatever she liked while she was the Queen's guest and could see Her Majesty when and how she liked. Immediately after the burial, Wallis wanted to return to Paris and told the Queen she "felt ill" and wanted "to go home." In an interview quoted in Ralph Martin's biography, the Queen asked Wallis why she wanted to leave "at once." Wallis' simply responded: "Because I want to go." It was as if being accepted as a member of the family after thirty-six years of being shunned certainly did not give Wallis any reason or desire to seek out additional exposure. In a way, I imagined, Wallis was spontaneously being even more regal than the Queen.

Once again my fantasies about history were interrupted by reality and Christina's dinner. Like at the gala earlier that year, Wallis made certain we would arrive late for the party and leave early. We sat at a large table with Christina and our hostess's younger friends. During the entire dinner, Wallis spoke less than she had in the fifteen minute drive from her home to the restaurant.

It would be a year later, after Christina's father's death, that I saw Christina again for a very difficult last meeting at the International Hospital.

The Duchess of Windsor in Switzerland circa 1958

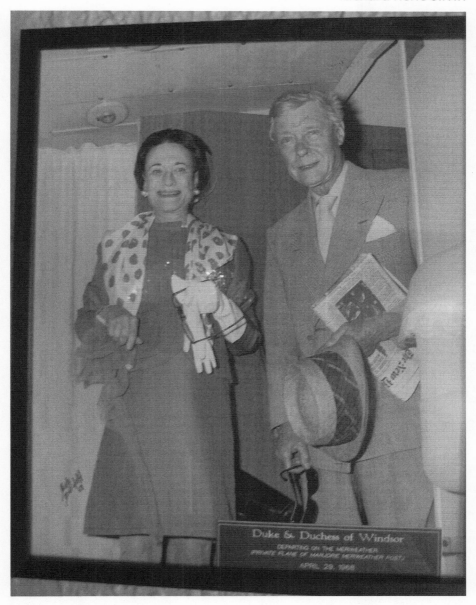

The Duke and Duchess boarding Marjorie Merryweather Post's plane,

"The Merryweather"

frail Duchess and an elegant Miss Schutz disembarking the Rafaello with an aging

Black Diamond and another pug, 1975

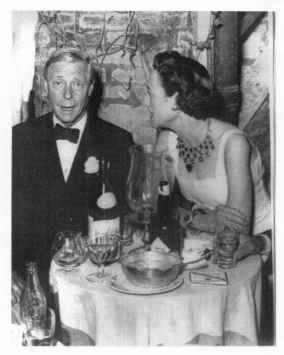

The Duke and Duchess of Windsor, Venice Italy, circa 1954

The Windsors' in Palm Beach, Florida, 1964

Queen Elizabeth visits her dying uncle at Le Boise accompanied by Prince Philip
and Prince Charles May 17, 1972

At the Duke's funeral, Frogmore, Windsor With Queen Elizabeth and Prince Philip
June 5, 1972

The Duchess following the Duke's funeral, "Because I want to go."

Part Five

GREAT PEOPLE OFFER ADVICE

&

WALLIS' REPUTATION

IN THE 70'S

Chapter 1

AT LE BOIS

Georges, the butler, met me at the door. Great British empire-era butlers were called by their last names, but the Windsors used a less formal terminology and called their head butler by his first name of Georges. The Duchess had recently and abruptly dismissed one long tenured butler the Duke had hired while serving in the Bahamas. Sidney Johnson had worked for the royal couple for almost thirty years. The two men, butler and master, were inseparable. Perhaps Wallis wanted to remove any reminders of that era in her life, and "Johnson" clearly did so. Luckily, several decades later, Mohamed Al Fayed rehired an elderly Johnson to, once again, be the butler at the famous house.

"That sounds rather interesting, René," said the Duchess. "But why does the hospital need another Board? And how will that differ from the actual Board of Governors?" During lucid moments, Wallis possessed a keen mind and clearly wanted to learn what she thought were modern hospital concepts. She was using a lunch at her home for this series of questions and was dressed in a light blue silk dress, silk stockings, and of course beautiful jewelry including what became a famous piece when auctioned many years later: her peacock pin.

"Well, Duchess," I began to answer her questions and address the reason for my invitation, "all hospitals need a connection to their communities..." I paused when I saw her touch her forehead and take on a blank look.

"Are you feeling poorly?" I asked.

She immediately returned to the subject and the present conversation:

"Oh, no, I am fine. You were saying?" she said forcing a laugh.

"The current Board of Governors represents the Franco-American community and is closely linked to the American Embassy, the American Cathedral and American business in Paris - all American. There really is no representation by well-connected French people. I feel that it could be very helpful as the hospital goes through a transition to a genuinely modern, up to date hospital with French people representing us."

"But do you *really* feel it is not – 'up to date'?" asked Wallis somewhat bewildered.

"Not only do I feel it is not up to date, but I fear that both the hospital and even the individual board members may be at some risk of negligence."

"Negligence?" she asked, raising her voice and frowning which often caused her eyebrows to come together. "What on earth do you mean? Don't they do their best?"

It was clear she was not thinking of herself or any risk she may have. The Duchess was always in a separate, almost sacred category! Then she became pensive and added: "It has been suggested that they missed the Duke's cancer until it was far too late. What a senseless loss if that is so." Her voice trailed off.

I felt uncomfortable with her profound and honest concern and, sadly in retrospect, chose to return to the issue at hand.

"Unfortunately, 'their best' may be inadequate."

Wallis leaned forward and elevated her strong chin, as she did when she wanted explanations.

"You have to remember," I continued, "that we are an International Hospital, funded by the American State Department and recognized by the American Hospital Accreditation boards. As such we have to comply with American procedures and standards."

"But that's what you are doing and that's what gets silly Cheek all upset, is it not?"

"That is a part of it. We need to go much further and to establish links to influential French people who can come to our rescue politically by refuting some rather valid rumors circulating the city about how we have become, well… medically inferior."

Wallis gazed off at the beautiful garden and the woods beyond. This was her look of concentration again and not the confusion I would periodically see and come to hate.

As we moved into the dining room, I assumed she was thinking about details of their visits to the hospital during the diagnosis and treatment of the Duke's cancer. I had flashes of how they must have listened intently to – perhaps less than competent – physicians giving them the same horrendous news that all "ordinary" families get when facing such catastrophes. Social status or royalty does not lessen – or impact – the worry, sadness, fear and grief of such situations. In fact it magnifies the isolation that these periods create. From what I knew of the Duke, he was usually mild tempered and passive. Surely, Wallis had to be the one in control during the illness and her exposure to, and knowledge of, medical matters was unfortunately limited. I assume the horrible, eighteen month long experience is what motivated the Duchess to do "her bit" by actively serving on the International Hospital's board.

The dining room was set up for the two of us at a rectangular table for eight. The chairs were in light blue wood with white damask upholstery. For larger, formal parties, the Duchess had the room rearranged to hold three round tables of eight.

"You can keep one conversation flowing with eight at a table," she once said. "That is not possible when ten people are gathered together."

The layered curtains were blue with some gold trim and the walls were covered with dark panels depicting Chinese scenes. I wondered if Wallis held "dark" albeit important memories of her years in China.

Even in the company of a less important guest like I, when eating in the dining room Wallis had her gold pen and pad set beside her place. It had been her habit during the several decades as Duchess that she recorded small observations of imperfection during the service of a meal. These notes ranged from the quality of the food or the spices used, to the decoration on and setting of the table. The staff was used to being reeducated on her likes and dislikes after every meal which had included guests. Wallis was definitely a hands-on hostess and left no detail up to interpretation by the staff. Today, she sat at the head of the single table and I was placed in the middle of the side to her right.

I had overcome my bedazzlement about being of interest to her. Luckily, and perhaps, because I was too young and naive to even realize the huge privilege I was being offered. I began to wonder how someone in her position, and given her history, wanted to understand the specifics of a rather tedious subject like modern hospital administration. I remember clearly that at that exact moment, I found her to be quite amazing. This was not a superficial lady. She was isolated by circumstance and history, but underneath, she was curious and intelligent – ready to engage. And, contrary to public opinion, she was animated and charming. Once we were seated, each having had our respective chairs held by separate butlers, she picked up the train of thought.

"But what do you mean by 'negligent'?" she repeated, indicating that her mental lapses were only occasional. It was she who picked up the thread of the lost conversation.

"The Board cannot claim ignorance for what is going on in the hospital. In an odd way we have opened Pandora's box by creating this new managerial assessment. By making the Board aware of how we feel, we have also created, in them, an implied sense of duty to do the right thing. Hospitals in America are increasingly victims of lawsuits – some frivolous, but all painful to the defendants, nevertheless. And many members of *this* Board are so famous; I fear a well publicized law suit in the United Sates against us, for an overt act of malpractice could be sensational and very damaging."

"Fascinating," said Wallis with a genuine air of interest and concern. "Who do you want to be on this committee and will Perry support this? I like the name Perry. A former Perry was a very close friend."

Wallis was referring to Perry Brownlow who she had met at the Fort shortly before the abdication. He escorted her during the harrowing trip as they fled England. He sat patiently with Wallis' aunt Bessie while Wallis hurriedly scribbled out her last will and testament in case she did not reach France safely; such was the level of fear Wallis experienced in those final days in England.

"And are you not further alienating the physicians?" she continued.

I was impressed at the Duchess' political acumen in forecasting another potential conflict with the medical staff.

"The doctors will not be happy," I said "because they are never happy unless they are the very center of attention and activity. This committee will place yet another level of importance above them and one that will indirectly impact them over time. If the group is thoughtfully chosen, it will be a huge support to us in Paris. Perry is all for it."

"And who will you ask to join?"

"Perry thinks that Jean-Jacques Guerlain should chair the committee," I explained.

"I know him, of course, but not well," said the Duchess.

"He is arguably the only 'real Frenchman' in the current group. That is why we chose him. We hope he will take on the added responsibility of helping us recruit an appropriate French team of well connected Parisians."

Wallis wanted to talk about Guerlain. "We did not see him very often, but he is a gentleman and quite a legend actually. Shalimar was always my favorite perfume. I've used it for ages. Such a subtle and classic scent! You know it was developed in 1925 as part of the decorative arts movement? And Vol de Nuit, your mother's fragrance. It came later."

The Duchess referred to two of the more than three hundred scents that the House of Guerlain had developed. Once again, I was amazed that she remembered such a detail about my mother and was eager to explain perfume history to me. She became pensive again and continued:

"Tell Perry it is a good choice. Guerlain is much respected. He is a good friend of Genevieve so I suggest you let her know. Noblesse oblige, René!" Wallis clearly felt that it was my duty to inform the proper people to avoid criticism.

As often the case during my meetings with Wallis, I was exceptionally impressed that this iconic woman, who had lived a totally secluded life in the highest levels of society, was interested in many different subjects. Also, her request for me to inform one of the other Grande Dames of Paris was indicative of her well-developed sense of social politics and proper diplomacy. I was fortunate enough to have met other women in the Duchess' circle of 'friends' and, for the most part, did not find a similar thirst for details and understanding of events other than their areas of immediate concern – usually fashion, travel or society. Sadly, because Wallis was so venerated and also feared, it was hard for her to know exactly which "friends" were loyal and genuinely desirous of being with her. Most acquaintances only wanted to be seen – and even better photographed – with her. These circumstances may have been tolerable - even amusing - while the Duke was alive but it was extremely difficult for her in the mid 1970's. I'd like to think I challenged her mind at this critical point in her life.

I wondered what she might have been able to accomplish with her means and position if she had been directed towards business and more charities. She had developed a fear of politics due to previous scandals. I believe her somewhat inept forays into politics were the direct result of having been harshly ostracized by the British Royal family. Clearly, going to Germany shortly after their wedding was imprudent and misguided, but people like the Windsors did not employ publicists or consultants in those days. They were who they were and if bad publicity ensued, they wondered why the world mis-understood them. Ironically, no one dared explain the reasons for negative public reactions. The famous and outwardly sophisticated couple was quite *unsophisticated* in this regard.

However, at the onset of her dementia and in her lonely state of being widowed, I could see a deep curiosity for relevant details and an admirable sense of both duty and kindness to a young protégée.

The Duke and Duchess of Windsor at Le Bois, circa 1970

The Duke is holding Black Diamond who stayed on the Duke's bed the night he died May 22, 1972

The Duke's Bedroom at Le Bois with the Order of the Garter above the bed

Chapter 2

JEAN-JACQUES GUERLAIN

Within a few days, Perry and I went to meet Jean-Jacques Guerlain. Guerlain had been a "part–time" board member and we were not sure if he would be willing to accept the mission we were about to propose. This request would require a much broader and direct role and, importantly, a significant amount of time and thought. In contrast to the Duchess or Genevieve's family, Guerlain was not considered 'royalty' or 'of lineage', but the family was admired and respected for its history, wealth and reputation.

The famous "perfumery" was created in 1828 by the Jean-Jacques' great grandfather and had been run by Guerlains ever since. It was one of the oldest and most respected businesses of its type and, in the 1970's, was still independent. During the entire century that preceded my meeting Monsieur Guerlain, the company had enjoyed a very loyal following of socialites around the world. A Guerlain perfume was considered by many as a status symbol and, consequently, what we now call brand loyalty was very strong.

The family had a tradition of not only producing delightful and distinctive scents but also for selling in a time when sophisticated marketing methods were rarely understood. As the Duchess had informed me, her perfume, Shalimar, had been produced to honor the decorative arts movement. Vol de Nuit, my late mother's perfume, was launched to revere the great French author and philosopher: Antione de Saint Exupery who wrote the delightful, yet profound, children's book called *Le Petit Prince* (The Little Prince).

Jean-Jacque's father, Jacques, had run the company for several decades. The older Guerlain worked closely with *his* grandson, Jean-Paul. It is said that the younger Guerlain generations had "inherited the Guerlain nose." They ventured into colognes for men, notably the hugely successful Vetiver. While it was Jean-Paul who inherited the "nose," they all inherited the Guerlain fortune, sense of style and respected name.

Some twenty years later, the Guerlain family would sell the company to Louis Vuitton Moet Hennessy. LVMH, as it is known in publicly traded corporate circles, was, and is an enormous concern and part of France's "CAC 40" roughly the equivalent of the New York Stock exchange's Dow Jones Industrials. Adding the Guerlain name to the long list of companies owned by LVMH was strategically in line with making and selling the very best brands. The transaction made the Guerlain family into billionaires.

Jean-Jacques was in his early seventies. He had piercing eyes, thinning grey hair and a kind face. Slightly overweight, exceptionally distinguished and chic, he dressed impeccably, of course, and always wore a suit, often three pieces with a vest. In his left lapel he proudly displayed the small red button; indication that he had received the French Legion of Honor – the highest decoration awarded to Frenchmen.

We met at the Travelers Club on the Champs Elysees, the widest boulevard in Paris which leads up to the Arc of Triumph. After a pre-lunch glass of sherry in the beautiful club's drawing room, we proceeded to the dining room where Perry began:

"Jean-Jacques, we feel that the hospital needs better and broader French representation."

"I couldn't agree more," answered the eminently elegant man. "In fact, I have thought this for some time."

He paused momentarily as he immediately understood the whole purpose of our meeting added: "I hope you do not expect *me* to head this committee?"

"Yes, I sincerely hope so," continued Perry. "You are highly respected throughout Europe and frankly, your name will allow us to attract people of similar distinction."

"Flattering, yes, but I am not able to dedicate much time to this."

"We will do all the leg work," I interjected hopefully. "We will look to you only for important tasks. For example, we hope you will appoint and approve other members and you will chair the meetings which we will only call twice a year."

"Mmm," responded Guerlain somewhat cynically and implying that he had embarked on other missions that allegedly would not take "much" of his time.

A good bottle of Bordeaux coupled with a great meal and conversation gradually brought a smile to Guerlain's face. By the time we parted ways, I scratched out a few names Jean-Jacques mentioned on a piece of paper. They included five members of the French nobility: a Countess, three Barons and one Count. Also included were four other Frenchmen who had earned the Legion of Honor.

"Do you think Homer Deberry would make a suitable member?" asked Perry as I took notes on who would speak to whom.

"Yes, of course he would. But let us not be naïve. As President of the French Senate I rather doubt he will accept."

Perry looked at me and winked. I had related every detail of my little "chat" at the mayor's office which concluded with Deberry offering to be part of the undertaking if we "reached an understanding" about our receivable.

"I think he will," I added. "In fact, he has already indicated a willing-ness to serve."

Then fearing I may have shocked Guerlain and somehow lessened his authority, I added:

"Assuming you were in agreement that such a committee should be created. If you like, I will confirm this with him. And, I'd also very much like your approval to ask another person to help us."

"Who is that," asked Guerlain gently.

"Doctor Charles Mérieux."

Again Guerlain expressed his concern that the head of the huge pharmaceutical giant that bore his family name and was about to be acquired by Rhone-Poulenc, a French conglomerate, would never want such a responsibility. Later the combined company became Sanofi-Aventis, the third largest pharmaceutical company in the world.

"The takeover must be all consuming," said Guerlain. "And he has already created an important foundation and a new and separate pharmaceutical company called Bio-Mérieux."

"Yes that is all true, but I know him well," I said as mildly as possible, fearful of sounding like "a young upstart." I could see Guerlain was curious as to how and why this was the case.

"My family has been close friends of the Mérieux family for generations. Doctor Mérieux has been a kind, generous and invaluable advisor to me. He was responsible for choosing my company to design a private hospital in Lyon. And we have consulted with Bio-Mérieux regarding the creation of an advanced health-screening unit at their new offices. I think the expression 'if you want something done, ask a very busy man' applies to him. May I ask him?"

Suddenly, Guerlain was both impressed and motivated to further the challenge. Guerlain became deep in thought and said:

"I'll need a powerful friend to help me. I am thinking of His Excellency Hervé Alphand. Alphand had been France's ambassador to the United States from 1956 to 1966 and was still well connected to inner circles of government in both countries.

"He as well as others you suggest will all be included," said Perry.

We concluded our meeting in the most amiable of fashions and I raced back to the hospital to call Genevieve and ask to see her. I would not forget my pledge to the Duchess nor to the importance of diplomacy. After all it was Genevieve who coined the phrase "the shark tank" and I knew we were about to create more intrigue.

Chapter 3

THE HOME OF GENEVIEVE ACHILLE-FOULD PRAY

Marcel, the loyal butler in his usual white jacket, met me at the huge double doors and led me up the wide marble stairs to the main drawing room where I had last seen Genevieve. I thought that a horse could have walked up these stars and wondered if Napoleon had done exactly that. It was rumored that the Emperor did indeed ride his horse up the stairs of some select friends' homes around Paris and this historic residence had been in the family during his reign. Somehow the Achille Fould's, like the great Talleyrand, had managed to be prominent ministers in the conflicting and successive French governments: the monarchy, the Empire, the subsequent transition governments and even into the era of the five successive French Republics.

Marcel knocked and without waiting opened the doors and stood back indicating that I should enter. The elegant woman was alone and I had the odd feeling that she spent a great deal of time alone, in her "golden cage" caressing her little, white dog. Her broad smile seemed quite genuine and she indicated that I should sit in an armchair near her. Again, I could not avoid seeing the huge "knuckle to knuckle" emerald ring she wore. It was quite evident as she gently caressed her lucky dog.

After asking me if I'd like anything to drink and then dismissing Marcel, she said:

"I am pleased that you have asked to see me."

"Actually, Madame," I answered, "it was the Duchess who recommended it. Of course, I was delighted that she did." While there was more than one Duchess in Genevieve's circle, only one could be identified as "the" Duchess.

I certainly did not want this Hollywood picture of a great lady to be insulted.

"How is Wallis? You know we all worry about her."

The inference to her failing mind was clear. "I find her to be very well, Madame. Of course life as a widow is not easy. I had lunch with her at Le Bois recently."

"What a lovely and comfortable home. Do you know that there is a small dining room upstairs between their two bedrooms? They ate there often – alone in their last years."

To Genevieve, Le Bois was "comfortable" and not grand as her Chateau de Beychevelle, but, then again, nothing is.

"I have not been upstairs, but I know the ground floor and the kitchen below."

Genevieve went on: "The Duke and she were very close, you know. Sam and I were lucky to be considered amongst their friends. They were quite a team all those years, really. And they had loads of fun traveling and dancing together at all the popular clubs. In the early days, they brought as many as one hundred and twenty pieces of luggage on the ships when they went to America twice a year. Cunard eventually had to gently tell them that it was a strain on the crew! Can you imagine? When he was ill, she cared for the Duke and never left his side. Now she is alone. It is said that she sees very few people."

I realized, yet again, how lucky I was to be one of those "very few people."

She continued: "Frankly, I blame the hospital. His cancer was detected far too late and they did not consult other physicians when his symptoms first appeared! Finally, the Duchess had an expert fly in from New York who confirmed that the Duke's cancer had progressed and was beyond being treatable. By the time the American specialist saw the Duke, there was nothing that could be done for the poor man. It is said that those who had a great love are very fortunate. I'm sure that is true. But what happens when one is left alone?"

"I cannot imagine how difficult it is for her right now." My youthful mind clumsily answered, "But, again, it was she who suggested I speak to you about the hospital."

It was not necessary to add which hospital – that, too, was obvious.

"And what is the subject at hand?" asked Genevieve.

"We are about to create a new and separate Board. We plan to call it 'The French Advisory Committee.' The Duchess felt that you should be informed and consulted before it becomes known."

"I am flattered," said Genevieve as she stroked the fortunate pooch. After a short pause, she added,

"Is she really concerned about such issues?"

"Yes, Madame," I answered. "She is and asks for information frequently."

"You are a lucky man. May I call you René?" Without an answer, she continued. "You may not yet understand just how lucky you are to be exposed to her. I hope you appreciate the privilege. One day you will come to know exactly how great this lady is and what her life has been – what she has had to endure with public opinion and gossip. Imagine, in love with the King of England and then marrying him after the abdication! Then thirty six-years together. It is more than one can understand at your age."

"I try to," I answered inaccurately. In fact I had no idea of the enormous fortune which I was living, although I did recognize how great and unique the Duchess' life had been. To be closely involved in one of the Duchess' last great areas of interest was indeed a huge stroke of good luck.

"What do you expect of me, exactly?" asked Genevieve.

"The Duchess simply wants you to be informed so that you may head off any discomfort that the medical staff may have."

Genevieve smiled. "I don't think you have to worry about Cheek on *that* subject. With the Duchess on your side his attacks are neutralized. I'd be more worried about her health and…." She paused for quite a long period before she resumed, "I'm not sure I should go further."

"That's up to you Madame, but I can assure you of my discretion."

"Very well," continued Genevieve. "There is a much bigger storm brewing at that shark tank you are trying to pull together." Again, she paused, this time collecting her thoughts and preparing her explanation. "You are close with Perry, is that correct?"

"Yes, Madame," I answered. "He has been a generous friend and great mentor to me. Without his diplomatic intervention, I may well have lost my job last year."

"And the Duchess," said Genevieve. "Do not forget her! But there is this other sensitive matter at hand. Are you aware of Perry's double life?"

Now it was I who paused and tried to collect my thoughts. I certainly was not about to betray Perry but, clearly, the word of his affair with the exquisite Patricia was "out" and appeared to be creating the exact controversy Perry feared.

"Your silence indicates that you do, René" continued Genevieve. "You know Harriet is highly respected by the more traditional elements of the Board and the Franco-American community. Many are very upset and rallying to her side. They have linked you and Perry together as a team and, some feel, it would be best to rid the hospital of you both simultaneously."

"But that makes no sense," I said.

"Of course it does not make sense," said Genevieve sourly, a little irritated. "But it is a fact. Cheek and Chevalier understood that they needed more ammunition and they now have rallied a whole new group who want to attack on moral grounds. They even intend to involve the Dean of the American Cathedral and the Ambassador. Frankly, I am worried for you because of this new approach to – as they call it – 'solve all the problems at once.'"

"But that is so primitive and unjust," I almost begged, as if she needed convincing.

"I am on your side, don't forget. The opposition also claims that you arrange for – let's call them – special favors to the Congressional Chairman. That is how they worked you into the moral picture. I could care less what entertainment you have to provide Passman. In fact I admire the ingenuity! And it is none of our business what Perry does or who he loves. Only hypocrites focus on those things. Do you know the girl?"

"Yes, quite well," I answered wondering how red my face had become following the mention of Passman's name and our extracurricular activities, "Patricia is simply remarkable. Perry seems to have regained his lost youth and the two of them are a marvelous team. She is as charming and capable as she is beautiful. I'd do anything to see the relationship prevail."

"Well, it is clear that it is all coming to a head. I will do my best to help you both. The French committee is not your problem and could, in fact, be a help. Who are the members?"

"Jean-Jacques Guerlain has agreed to be the Chairman."

"That's impressive," she said. "Who else?"

"We are still putting the full list together. But Count Guy de Carmoy, Baron Alain de Gunzburg, Baron Guy de Rothschild…."

"Excellent," she said. "He will help and I know him well. And de Gunzburg also being Jewish has a lot in common with my family. De Gunzburg and de Carmoy are closely associated with the Bronfman family and again we have a lot in common as we both produce liquor. And…?"

"The Countess de Vogue…"

"She loves theater. Please go on."

"Baron Hottinguer…"

"The Swiss bankers," said the all-knowing Genevieve.

"Homer Deberry," I pressed on.

"I find that one hard to believe," she said inquisitively.

"I know, Madame, but it is true. Perhaps he is more interested in the future of his city than we thought."

Genevieve threw her head back and laughed cynically while she waited for more names.

"Yves Lanvin, Bernard Francois-Poncet…"

"Good God. This is a list of *Who's Who* in Paris. Unbelievable. Lanvin and Guerlain – the two huge competitors working together! That is wonderful. And the great Francois-Poncet will have no opposition. You know his father was a young dandy and served as Ambassador to Germany shortly before the outbreak of the war. But there are some names you mentioned who are puritans and consider themselves moral beacons. God only knows what skeletons are in *their* closets."

I was suddenly nearly in love with this grand lady. I had no idea how liberal and pragmatic she was. I continued down the nearly completed list and was not interrupted again until I got to Charles Mérieux.

"Now *that* is a fantastic story – the world renowned Charles Mérieux. Are you aware that he inoculated the entire country of Brazil when no one thought it could be done? He chartered 747's from Air France and loaded them with vaccines and personnel. And he went along to personally supervise. "

"Yes, I am informed about the Brazilian accomplishment. I know him well and admire him very much. He and his father discovered the hoof and mouth vaccine, the tetanus vaccine and others."

"Indeed," said Genevieve. "Well, back to the shark tank: I will tell you I love a good fight. Before our discussion, I thought both you and Perry might well have to retire together. But now, it will never happen, at least if I have my way. Let's speak periodically. You have my word, I will do my best. But I strongly recommend Perry bring the matter out in public."

After some lighter conversation, I excused myself and was escorted to the sidewalk by Marcel. I had to find Perry as soon as possible.

Chapter 4

HEART TO HEART WITH PERRY

"Can we meet out of the hospital?" I asked Perry.

"Yes, how about drinks at the Travelers Club."

We were back at the great town home of Madame de Maintenon, where she entertained "The Sun King," Louis XIV. When we were comfortably seated I got ready for a rather *uncomfortable* conversation.

"I have spoken to the Duchess and Genevieve," I began. "Both are totally supportive of the French advisory board. But Genevieve brought up another matter which may be of greater concern than the medical staff or even raising the necessary money to add to the building fund."

"What's that?"

"Well…." Before I could finish he said:

"Shit. Don't tell me Genevieve brought Patricia up."

"Yes, sadly she and – it seems – all of Paris is aware."

"Christ," he said expressing deep concern.

"Perry, if everyone knows you are concealing the relationhip they can criticize you for what even the advanced Genevieve called 'a double life'. She felt, and I must say I agree, that you have to come clean one way of the other and now."

"No question," answered Perry. "I have wanted to rent a flat in Neuilly and have Patricia move in anyway. I want to divorce Harriet and try to finally have a family with Patricia."

"Why that's wonderful," I exclaimed. "But sooner rather than later, please. Cheek intends to speak to the Dean."

"The little weasel," exclaimed Perry.

"It gets worse, my friend."

"That would be hard to believe," said Perry now deep in thought.

"Well, it does. They know about the… procurements we make for Passman. It seems that you and I are both branded as 'immoral' among these hypocrites. We are lumped together. And, Perry, I have still another problem."

"Heap it on," he said breaking the trance with some laughter.

"Well things are deteriorating in Washington. I may have to go back according to what the bank told me."

"Not on your life! And certainly not before the management study and the architectural drawings are complete. That would really do me in."

"They will both be finished this winter. I'd never leave before that but it may happen after. Now, for some good news."

"Thank God," said Perry.

"This month's financials will finally show us in the black. It seems that the cost cutting measures are working. No one can criticize us on that score especially given the many years of losses."

"Terrific. I'd better go and speak with Patricia and look into renting that flat. We'll be neighbors and I look forward to that. This will certainly create a huge ruckus around town. Maybe history will be kind to us; unlike it has been to Wallis."

Perry Culley

Chapter 5

WALLIS' REPUTATION IN THE 1970'S

After the Duke's death, Wallis' public appearances lessened in both importance and frequency. More important perhaps is that her conduct was exemplary albeit in a socialite context. No rational person could be critical of her behavior after 1972. She attended very few important events, notably those described in this story, but was always sober, elegant and, if anything, protective and reserved. Gone were the days when she may have engaged in late night excesses. Furthermore, Wallis only had a few years between the Duke's death and the onset of her own obvious dementia. It is likely that the onset of the disability began in 1972, around the time of her being widowed. A second phase of intermittent clarity mixed with confusion probably lasted until 1977, after which she rapidly became senile. Fortunately, Wallis was mostly clear-minded, albeit sad and lonely, during the time of the personal events which take place in this story.

Once widowed, Wallis' attorney, Suzanne Blum, became more and more influential in Wallis' life and in the conduct of her business affairs. "Maitre Blum" has been criticized for being overly protective – even abusive and dishonest. There is speculation that Maitre Blum turned her head as some treasures, both large and small, left Le Bois during the Duchess' long illness. Still other authorities are convinced that Maitre Blum significantly altered the Duchess' last will and testament after the Duchess was unable to make clear decisions for herself.

Unfortunately, however, Wallis' past continued to fuel numerous rumors, many of which were unfair at best. Some were pure fabrication. Theories abound about what really took place in 1936, while Edward was King of England, and in the two decades that followed. The most hurtful of these stories were never, and cannot ever, be proven. In spite of numerous books with conjecture, the accurate detail of these events went to the Royal graves of both Wallis and Edward at Frogmore Cemetery.

There were two serious – and one frivolous - subjects which were the basis of the political distrust and, eventually, dislike – even hatred - of Wallis. The somber subjects are her possible activities with Nazi Germany and her role in causing Britain to "lose" her King.

It is certain that Wallis was recruited by US Naval intelligence for relatively small acts of intelligence transfer and what might be called "espionage" in the 1920's. These efforts which took place in France, England and China consisted of engaging in a low level transfer of information during the interval between the two great wars. Most assuredly whatever she may have disclosed was for the benefit of the United States. However, this early education gave Wallis a sense of international affairs and, possibly, intrigues.

Once she was married to Ernest Simpson and living in London, during the late 1920's and early 1930's, she continued to have strong opinions about international affairs. It is crucial to note that most of England's "intelligencia" was not only pro-German in the early 1930's, but even pro-Nazi for the first several years of Hitler's regime. It was not until the mid to late 1930's that Winston Churchill's pleas to properly evaluate Hitler's military buildup took hold. As late as September 1938 – a year after the Windsors' much criticized trip to Germany –

Prime Minister Neville Chamberlain returned from Munich, Germany waving a letter from Hitler asserting non aggression in Europe which gave the British people a temporary sigh of relief. It was only after this diplomatic farce became an obvious falsehood that the vast majority of people began to understand Germany had become both expansionist and cruelly fascist. Sadly Edward's marriage to Wallis coincided with these events and only an extremely astute politician would have realized that a sea of change in Europe had taken place.

During the first half of the 1930's, Wallis was befriended by extremely pro-German social hostesses including Lady Sybil Colefax and Lady Emerald Cunard. She was also acquainted with then respected German officials like Germany's diplomat, Count Joachim von Ribbenthrop. In fact, supporting what was known as "appeasement," namely befriending the previously defeated Germany, was the fashionable thing to do until late 1937 – the year that Wallis and Edward married. There was a belief, especially among the British upper class, that Germany had been harshly punished with sanctions imposed at the Treaty of Versailles shortly after World War I. The proponents of appeasement thought that turning a blind eye on the ever increasing German violations of the treaty would balance the restrictive role Germany had been forced to accept. Once Wallis became closely involved with the Prince of Wales, she found him to be, like all her friends, a man who was a strong proponent of appeasement. More importantly, he had some close German relatives, frequently visited Germany for over twenty-five years and spoke fluent German. It was he, the debonair all knowing Prince, who should bear responsibility for Wallis' somewhat understandable, early support of Nazi Germany.

After the abdication, it can be argued they both practiced poor judgment in traveling to Germany. Although the war was still two years hence, it was becoming rare to find informed politicians who continued to believe that Germany might have a passive strategy in Europe. One must also remember that after the abdication, Edward, then The Duke of Windsor, felt horribly abused and shunned by his former family and *his* former government. This is not a justification of what was likely a pro-Nazi position but, rather an explanation. Once again, however, he bears more responsibility in their joint activities and verbal indiscretions than does Wallis who, at the time, was quite bleary eyed about being married to the former King of England.

The second cause of public hatred for Wallis also began in the mid 1930's and lasted four long decades. It was the British public's belief that Wallis "stole England's King." Once again, the vast majority of "blame" for the constitutional crisis in 1936 and the eventual abdication that December lay with His Majesty the King, not with Wallis. There is abundant documentation in letters that Wallis wrote home to her beloved Aunt Bessie that she was not pushing for an abdication. In fact, quite to the contrary, Wallis wrote the King suggesting that she "steal quietly away." But marriage at "any cost" was Edward's verbalized goal and not Wallis'. As the predicament escalated, Wallis repeatedly suggested she leave England; first offering to return to the United States, only after Edward rejected that proposal because it would be more difficult for him to reunite with her, she decided to escape and seek a safe harbor with her friends, the Rogers', in the south of France. During this period she was as close to a "nervous breakdown" as at any other point in her life and was certainly not a behind the scenes, conniving conductor of the plot. The conclusion, once again, is that Edward, not Wallis, deserves to be held primarily responsible for *his* abdication.

Finally it is of merit to briefly discuss the "frivolous" rumors that surrounded the Royal couple. This set of criticism centers around their possible sexual activities and Wallis' control over Edward when he was Prince, later King and, finally, Duke. What one knows is that Edward was shy and overly attached to his mother, Queen Mary. While he had several early liaisons with women, there is no evidence that these were passionate or even satisfying to Edward. This lack of documentation, however, is not surprising in and of itself as the Prince of Wales was discrete in discussing details of his sexual relationships. Wallis, on the other hand, had become an experienced sexual partner and while young was, in appearance and in behavior, somewhat severe and harsh. It is this odd mix that first attracted Edward to Wallis when she verbally reprimanded him on several occasions in public. Within a short period of time, the Prince waited on Wallis' every wish even falling to his knees, to the utter astonishment of any witness, to adjust her skirt or pick up an object she may have dropped. If this behavior extended into the alleged masochistic sexual activity will never be known, nor is it anyone's right to conjecture.

Once the subject of the couple's sexual activities was perceived as acceptable conversation, talk rapidly grew out of control and, on occasion, invasive and even insulting. The couple was accused of numerous ménages a trois intermittently with a third woman or a third man. Most of these supposed partners are mentioned in this story, but deliberately not identified as possible sexual partners. Once again, whatever really happened is now sealed off in their graves and for the purposes of historical record is irrelevant.

In conclusion, Wallis was hated far more than she deserved. Her public demeanor after their marriage was more passive than in earlier days. This is repeatedly reinforced in her mid 1950's memoirs. One could only "accuse" Wallis of being cleverer than Edward and of sharing or indulging his bad sense of timing, his occasional ill temper and his propensity to over indulge in frivolity.

Importantly, in 1937, no one believed that their union would last. Yet, quite to contrary, history has proven that Wallis stayed solidly by Edward's side, during thirty-six years: through good and bad times, numerous scandals, years of relative tranquility, his illnesses and eventual death. Happily for the former King, his final days took place at their home, Le Bois, where he was both loved and well looked after even in direct contradiction to the International Hospital's recommendation.

It is possible and appropriate to draw parallels between Wallis and Evita Peron. Both women were clever and ambitious. Both came from backgrounds which critics considered scandalous and which the two women managed to conceal and negate more or less successfully. The two icons became international stars, exercising innovative techniques and judgment while being imaginative. Importantly, no one would have predicted either one's achieved stature only a few years before their meteoric rise in position and fame. They loved fashion to a point where they left their permanent imprint on style and, finally, both caught the eye and captured the heart of their respective country's most influential man who married them while being heavily criticized. These men, Juan Peron and Edward VIII, then spent much of the rest of their lives doing their best to validate their wives' reputations and contributing to their influence.

During their entire life together, Edward gently but consistently demanded the impeccable service he received during his upbringing. Dining room tables had to be perfectly set with different ornaments and decorations each night. His personal belongings had to be gathered wherever he left them, flawlessly cleaned and replaced to their proper locations. As a chain smoker, he dropped ashes every-where - on tables and floors. He placed glasses, without coasters, on furniture and important documents, even while he was King looking at papers sent to him in the famous "red boxes." Wallis learned to over-look these potentially disturbing habits and learned how to provide her husband the luxuries in great, varying and specific detail. To the amazement of those close to the Windsors, it was thanks to Wallis' ingenuity and creativity that the famous couple was able to lead a life of enormous luxury.

Part Six

PROBLEMS CONVERGE

1975

&

ROYAL MEMOIRS

Chapter 1

ARISTOTLE ONASSIS

Aristotle Onassis' story is unique, beginning with his earliest years. His domineering father, Socrates Onassis, had sadistically installed an unusual sense of fight and ambition in his only son. As a very young man, Aristotle had bribed Turkish guards to get his father released from prison – a feat which did not even earn a "thank you" from his ailing, disciplinarian father. Obsessed to obtain his father's praise, Aristotle began his business career in Argentina where, using innovative techniques – partly eavesdropping on important businessmen's conversations – he began to amass a fortune.

A fascinating and bizarre series of intermarriages and competition laced with tragedies that surrounded the Greek shipping giants began upon Aristotle's return to Greece. At the age of forty-six, Onassis married Tina Livanos, the seventeen-year-old daughter of the previous, leading shipping mogul, Stavaros Livanos. Ari then began to rapidly build his own fleet of freighters and tankers and made his mark on shipping when he deduced that ever increasing quantities of oil would have to be moved from the major oil producing countries to those that consumed the oil, notably the United States. This concept may appear as an obvious conclusion now but, right after the Second World War, it was both novel and brilliant. The feat that catapulted Onassis to great fame and fortune was his invention of the super-tanker which made his profit margins on transoceanic oil transfers far greater than any of his competitors, including his father-in-law. He then transformed his smaller aging freighters into whaling ships which embarked on an illegal slaughter of thousands of whales off the South American coast.

Livanos, however, was still consolidating his own control of international shipping. His older, other daughter, Eugenia, married the second shipping competitor: Stavaros Niarchos. For a short period of time the three competitors, Livanos, Onassis and Niarchos, managed to balance their hugely competitive spirits splitting the fruits of a major international Greek shipping monopoly. Onassis and Tina had two children, first a son, Alexander in 1948, and then their daughter, Christina, two years later, in December of 1950.

During this period, Onassis' activities were spread between Greece, France and Argentina. He carefully created a complicated web of business activities designed to avoid taxes – always adhering to his main principle that "the only rule is that there *are* no rules." One of his rented residences was the Chateau de la Croe near Cannes, France: the previous home of the Duke and Duchess of Windsor. Unbeknownst to Ari, his archrival, Stavaros Niarcos, bough the Chateau and had the great pleasure of evicting his famous rival and tenant.

In 1953, Ari figured out a way to base his emerging empire out of the small tax haven, the Principality of Monaco. He secretly bought up a majority of the publicly traded corporation which owned most of Monte Carlo, the capital city of Monaco, which geographically are one in the same given that Monaco is the second smallest country in the world. Société des Bains de Mer et Cercle des Etrangers (The Sea Bathing and Foreigners Club, Inc.) owned the beautiful – albeit slightly run down – and profitable casino and many other important pieces of real estate. Once the secretive accumulation of stock was complete, Ari basically controlled Monaco and had tremendous influence over its young Prince Rainier. He prominently moored his 322-foot yacht, Christina, which was then the world's largest and most luxurious vessel, in Monaco's harbor. Aboard the enormous vessel he kept a Piaggio, an amphibious plane, which he used to whisk him and his famous, influential guests "anywhere in the world at the drop of a hat." The aircraft would later become the root cause of Ari's demise.

Shortly after Ari's move to Monte Carlo, his marriage to Tina began to dissolve when Onassis fell in love, and publicly courted Maria Callas, one of the most famous and dramatic opera singers. Unable to accept the indiscrete behavior of her husband, which, incidentally, Onassis thought was quite acceptable, Tina divorced Aristotle and, for a period of time, dedicated her life to their two children. In the meantime the "Golden Greek," Onassis, and "La Callas," as they were both respectively called, lived a life of extreme luxury and fantasy. Maria had one child, most likely with Onassis, in 1960. Historians differ on whether Maria suffered a late stage miscarriage or the baby was stillborn. However, she quickly returned to the opera and resumed their highly visible, societal role. Only a few other couples were equally sought after, gossiped about and photographed. These included the tumultuous marriages and divorces of Elizabeth Taylor and Richard Burton, the escapades of the Duke and Duchess of Windsor and the Bouvier sisters: Jackie Kennedy and Princess Lee Radziwill.

During the summer of 1963 an unusual situation developed with the Bouvier sisters. Jackie was pregnant for the fourth time and

President Kennedy was beginning the reelection campaign for his second term. Since Jackie was unable to travel, the President invited his sister-in-law, Lee, to join him on an official visit to Germany. It is believed that this upset Jackie for two reasons: being left alone during her pregnancy and because overseas trips were her happiest times as First Lady. Therefore, it is likely she bitterly resented her sister going on the German trip. Alone, Jackie delivered a premature son, Patrick, on August 7, 1963. The unfortunate infant died two days later. Within weeks, Onassis invited Jackie to join him and several other guests including his then-mistress, Jackie's sister, on a cruise aboard the Christina. Although the President and his brother, Bobby Kennedy, strongly objected, Jackie's mind was made up. She accepted the invitation, conceding only that she would try to be as discrete as possible and avoid photographers to the best of her, and Onassis' ability. Consequently her departure from Washington was not publicized and she secretly boarded the yacht eluding the paparazzi. The ruse did not last long as pictures of Jackie aboard the vessel were taken with long range lenses. There were additional close-up pictures of the famous First Lady strolling along with Onassis on various Greek islands which were flashed around the world – eerily reminiscent of King Edward VIII and Wallis Simpsons' 1936 Mediterranean cruise aboard the Nahlin. Most society watchers believe that Jackie replaced her sister as Onassis intimate companion during this holiday.

Upon her return to Washington, Jackie agreed to accompany the President on the fatal, late November, 1963 campaign trip to Dallas. Only days later, Onassis flew to Washington for President Kennedy's funeral and was a great solace and companion to Jackie. In the following year (1964), Jackie dated a number of famous men including

Onassis and the International Hospital of Paris's architect, John Warnecke.

The ever competitive and ambitious Ari set his sights on befriending, dating and later marrying the "most famous woman of the world."
During this time it appears that he had stopped seeing Lee Radziwill. The attraction for Jackie was not only Onassis' great wealth and
extravagant lifestyle but also the very real belief that Onassis could
better protect Jackie and her children than the American security
detail that is assigned to former Presidents' widows. Jackie consulted
her brother-in-law, Bobby Kennedy, who begged Jackie to postpone
any further public display of her relationship with the infamous, even
notorious, Onassis until his own bid for the American presidency was
complete. While Jackie reluctantly agreed, she immediately and more
fervently returned to her plan of marrying Onassis following Robert
Kennedy's assassination on June 5, 1968. She made her famous statement "they are killing Kennedy's" and accepted Onassis' proposal for
marriage after a complex financial agreement had been negotiated.
Jackie married the billionaire on Skorpios, Onassis' private island
retreat in the Ionian Sea, on October 20, 1968.

Surprisingly, in 1971 Tina married her former brother-in-law, Ari's
always persistent rival, Stavaros Niarchos, in spite of the fact that
Niarchos had previously been married to Tina's own sister, Eugenia.
That marriage had ended catastrophically when Eugenia died on
Niarcos' private island of Spetsopoula in September of 1970. Due to
Ari's assertion that Eugenia was murdered, her cause of death has
remained controversial even to this day. Although the official cause
of death is listed as "overdose of barbiturates" three conflicting autop-
sies revealed a ruptured spleen and crushed throat. The most likely
cause of death is that Eugenia took an overdose after Niarcos had a

troubling conversation with his former wife, Charlotte Ford, an heiress to the Ford Motor Company. When Niarcos discovered Eugenia's unconscious body he probably exerted unreasonable force trying to revive her. A postscript to Eugenia's sad story is that the Niarcos/Ford marriage took place *while* Eugenia believed she was still married to Niarcos who had declared his marriage to Eugenia invalid. He eventually reconsidered and divorced Charlotte Ford to re-marry Eugenia.

By the early 1970's, Ari was having his own marital problems with Jackie. His obsession with her fame, during which he showered her with extraordinary gifts, began to wane. Following an ostentatious buying binge of jewelry, antiques and clothes, Jackie began spending more and more time in New York away from Onassis who, in turn, began spending more and more of his time with his former lover, Maria Callas, and his own two children, Alexander and Christina. December of 1971 was troublesome for Ari because his jet exploded on its final approach to Nice airport on the French Riviera. A few weeks later, Ari's close confidant, David Karr, had a similar scare when his yacht, The Asmeda Hope, blew up and sank in the harbor at Cannes, France.

Throughout 1972 Ari, Karr and his close business associate, Costa Gratsos, worked on two major projects. The first was to build a luxury harbor and embark on a major development of Haiti with the hope of turning the impoverished, corrupt island-country into a new Caribbean tax heaven – a replay of his having transformed Monte Carlo into a luxurious tax haven twenty years earlier. The second was to build a major oil refinery in Greece so that Onassis would have a vertical monopoly on oil transportation, refining and sale.

The tragic turning point in Ari's life took place on January 22, 1973 when his beloved son, Alexander's, plane crashed. Alexander, an avid pilot, had hoped to consolidate the family airline, Olympic Airways, by merging it with Onassis' air taxi service between Athens and the Greek islands. The small feeder airline was run, in part, by Alexander who heroically saved many lives by transferring seriously ill patients, during inclement weather, from Greek islands back to Athens for hospitalization.

For some time, Alexander had argued that the Piaggio aircraft he flew and was also on the Yacht Christina, was outdated and danger- ous. Records indicate that Onassis may have been willing to accept his son's decision *after* one final transatlantic cruise scheduled for the win- ter of 1973. Because Ari had terminated his personal pilots, Alexander recruited two Americans to accompany the party aboard the Christina as she crossed the Atlantic to the Caribbean. Alexander ordered a com- plete overhaul of the aging Piaggio that was performed by mechanics at the Olympic airways maintenance facility in Athens. Surprisingly, the renovated plane was never checked out after the mechanics finished their replacement of numerous systems and before Alexander was to perform his test flight with the new, American pilots.

On the fateful Monday of January 22, 1973, Alexander seated Don McCusker, the proposed pilot, in the left seat as Alexander took the right seat – usually reserved for the co-pilot. He then placed Mac McGregor, the new co-pilot, behind him in a passenger seat. Imme- diately after takeoff from the Athens airport, the Piaggio veered to the right and when the pilot made the necessary rudder correction, the angle worsened and the plane crashed at the end of the runway. The two Americans were seriously injured but Alexander – seated on the side of the impact – was mortally wounded and brought to a hospital in Athens. Over the next twenty-four hours, Ari, Jackie, Tina, Christina, Alexander's fiancée, Baroness Fiona Thyssen-Bornemisza and two American physicians arrived at the hospital. By the following day it was determined that Alexander was brain dead and he was removed from life support and allowed to die. Onassis had a plastic surgeon "repair" his dead son's face and, accompanied by Jackie and Christina, brought him to Skorpios to be buried. When told that Greek law prohibited the burial in the small private chapel where he had married Jackie, Ari exercised his principal that "the only rule is that there are no rules" and buried Alexander adjacent to the chapel. He then ordered the chapel be expanded to encompass the grave.

An examination of the crumpled plane revealed that the aileron (rudder Cables) were inverted when they were poorly installed during the maintenance. Therefore any correction to the plane's angle after take-off would only have magnified the error instead of rectifying it. Ari was convinced that the Piaggio had been sabotaged and that Alexander had been murdered. He spent much of the rest of his life trying to prove his theory. This quest even included claiming that the innocent new pilot was an accomplice to the crime, which, in Ari's mind, had been masterminded by the CIA. This theory seems illogical because there were many other, more efficient ways to have assassinated Alexander and the idea leaves unanswered the question of why the alleged accomplice (the pilot) would have risked his own life during the plot. Undaunted, Ari offered one million dollars to anyone who would bring forth evidence to prove his theory and he made sure that Don McGregor was indicted for manslaughter and, after his release from the hospital, was detained in Athens during a long drawn out legal battle. While these extraordinary efforts ruined McGregor's life it also had a serious negative impact on Ari. His own physical and mental health deteriorated rapidly as did Christina's already shaky relationship with Jackie.

The divorce discussions between Jackie and Ari, which had begun prior to Alexander's death, were temporarily discontinued probably because Jackie's qualities in times of crisis had briefly consoled Ari. In spite of repeated efforts, the couple was never able to reach an agreement for a separation.

Left to right: Princess Grace of Monaco, Aristotle Onassis, Maria Callas, Prince Rainier, circa 1958

Jackie Kennedy leaving the Yacht Christina

with her children 1968

Alexander and Aristotle Onassis circa 1968

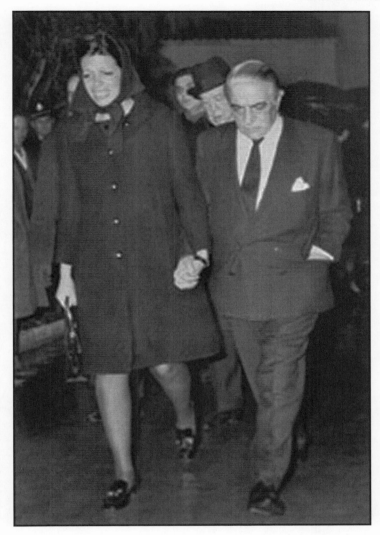

Christina and Aristotle Onassis after Alexander's funeral, 1973

Chapter 2

DEATH OF ARISTOTLE ONASSIS

During the last quarter of 1974, and I would like to think, due to our management changes and staff reductions at the International Hospital, the financial statements not only improved but the hospital reached a break-even point for the first time since they started to keep modern financial records. Perry had moved into a charming flat near us and was totally engrossed with his love for Patricia. She had decorated the apartment beautifully and placed the mementoes Perry had collected during his long and successful diplomatic career around the home. Had it not been for the fact that we knew the chief of staff was readying himself for a boardroom showdown, these would have been unthreatening and peaceful days.

One morning in early February, Perry summoned me to his office.

"René," he said, "I have just had a call from Aristotle Onassis' office. He is very ill and wants to come to the hospital."

I had seen pictures in the newspapers of Onassis walking in the Rue Royale in Paris with tape holding up his eyelids. It was widely believed in medical circles that Onassis suffered from Myasthenia Gravis, an autoimmune disease that causes the nerves and muscles to lose control. The name means "grave muscle weakness" in Greek. The result is that, as the illness progresses, the patient experiences fatigue, weakness and vision problems. In advanced cases, the victim develops difficulty in swallowing and, in the 1970's, the illness was often fatal once it affected the lungs.

"He is on his way to Paris from Greece now," continued Perry "and wants several rooms prepared for him and for his staff with new furniture and televisions. Do you think that can be done in two days?"

"Of course," I answered, "there is nothing easier. But why would he come here when we do not have a qualified neurologist or autoimmune specialist on staff? I have heard of a professor Drachman at Johns Hopkins who is leading the research for Myasthenia. So who will be his admitting physician here?"

"Christina brought a Parisian physician, Doctor Nicoli, to Greece to see her ailing father. It is Nicoli who recommended the family bring Onassis here. Since there appears to be some gallbladder involvement they have asked Chevalier to be his doctor. As to why they chose us, I'll be damned if I know why," answered a very excited Perry. "But he is coming and we'll do our best."

"But that's insane!" I exclaimed, "Chevalier is a general surgeon with high infection rates and is not competent to be the admitting doctor if Onassis has Myasthenia Gravis. He needs to go to Hopkins or, at the very least somewhere with an up-to-date neurologist on staff like New York or London if this acute phase is due to Myasthenia. Even if it is gallbladder related, he needs to be treated by a specialist other than the ones we have here."

"God help us," said Perry, "but Onassis is coming so let's make it as successful as possible. Now please call this aide to the Onassis family and work out the details."

Within minutes, I was speaking with Nico, a young secretary on Mr. Onassis' staff. Nico explained that they required four adjacent rooms at the end of any floor in the hospital – but it had to be at an end and Mr. Onassis' room would be the last one so as to assure privacy and silence. The other rooms, in order, were for a bodyguard, Christina and finally, one room set up as a sitting room for family and friends. Jackie who would accompany the party would not stay at the hospital. He explained that some furniture would be delivered by their Parisian staff. We were to provide a new hospital bed and furniture for Mr. Onassis and new regular size beds for Christina and the bodyguard. In addition, all televisions were to be replaced with new units as well as any other items that could be changed out in each room. The attention to Onassis' physical comforts was not unusual given the notoriety of the patient and I was used to similar requests.

I explained that changing the furniture and equipment was no problem as it could be done within a day. The cost would be added to their final bill. However, Nico had to understand that we were an acute care hospital and not a hotel. Given Mr. Onassis' status, we could allocate four rooms that would be billed as if each were occupied by an acutely ill patient. I went on to explain that such a patient who uses the hospital's facilities such as surgery, pathology and radiology usually commanded a "per patient day cost" of three times the room rate. Therefore, if they wanted to occupy the additional three rooms, they would be billed accordingly. All these details and a few others were immediately accepted.

"Do I assume that Mr. Onassis will be accompanied by personal physicians?" I asked.

"No," replied a surprised Nico. "We are coming to the International Hospital because Doctor Nicoli has recommended you and we know you will supply the necessary, well qualified physicians."

The answer shocked me then and still does to this day. I concluded that even the world's most influential and successful businessmen may be totally ignorant and poorly advised when it comes to healthcare. Worse, perhaps, is the thought that these people would never consider entering into a complex business venture without proper advice and counsel, probably confirmed by several sources. In matters of life and death healthcare, however, they might blindly run into the arms of an incompetent physician at a hospital that had little or no expertise with their specific diagnosis. Their attention to detail like furniture and luxury items would be meaningless and of no medical help regarding the ultimate outcome of the patient.

The same day a few patients were moved from the "Eisenhower wing" of the hospital with profound apologies and appropriate gifts in order to vacate four contiguous rooms. By the following day all physical adjustments to the rooms were made and they had been thoroughly cleaned. The evening news reported that the Onassis delegation and family had reached Paris and were ensconced in their Avenue Foch apartment. One television network showed a frail Onassis desperately trying to walk on his own from his limousine to the front door of the apartment building while Jackie and Christina stood nearby looking frightened and exhausted. The reporters theorized that Onassis was dying and returning to Paris – most likely – for the last time.

The following day, I met Jackie Kennedy Onassis and Christina Onassis at the hospital entrance. Christina's face was marked by fear and well-deserved concern. Jackie appeared calm and focused but Christina's cold attitude toward Jackie underscored her lack of affection for her famous mother-in-law. In order to avoid the large crowd of reporters, Onassis rode separately in a plain car and was brought to a basement entrance adjacent to, and used by, the morgue. His eyes were taped open and his breathing was labored.

Shortly after admission, which was conducted by aides and without the patient, Aristotle Onassis was seen by Professor Chevalier who recommended that Onassis' gallbladder be removed. To my knowledge no one asked what relationship the proposed operation had to Myasthenia Gravis or if new less invasive treatments in the United States for gallbladder problems had been considered. Although there was much less information about the relatively rare autoimmune condition in the 1970's, and certainly very few treatment options, the only gland known then (and now) that enters into the cause of the illness is the thymus. The thymus gland, located in the upper chest, is relatively large in infants and gradually atrophies with age. The gland controls the development of, and plays a large part in, the maintenance of the human immune system. In rare instances in modern medicine, the thymus gland is removed in untreated, late stages of Myasthenia Gravis. No research has ever revealed or even suggested that the gallbladder plays any role in the illness.

On Sunday, February 9th, Onassis had his gallbladder removed while his traveling entourage waited in their private lounge. I saw Christina after the surgery and everyone in the group was optimistic after their post-operative conference with Professor Chevalier. By now the party had expanded and several aides and lawyers routinely arrived and left, all crowded into the private sitting room.

Sadly, and almost predictably, by the second day after the operation, Onassis developed a serious infection. Initially the infection was confined to his lungs and our famous patient was treated with several, sequential courses of antibiotics over what seemed like an interminable period of over two weeks. At around this point in the stay, Jackie returned to New York. Christina seemed quite relived that she could now attend to her ailing father without interference. Shortly after Jackie left, Maria Callas came to visit the man she had loved for decades - and likely still did. From his sick bed, Ari tried to conduct business even pursuing Alexander's alleged assassination fourteen months earlier.

On one occasion, Christina came to my office in tears. I was as compassionate as possible, but I was unable to answer the obvious questions of why her father had to undergo surgery in the first place, why he had developed an infection and, importantly, why the infection had now worsened and had not been managed. She explained that Chevalier had also told Christina that her father's condition had gone from "stable" to "serious."

Morning television news shows had just begun in France, in 1975. I was watching one while I dressed the following day to go to the hospital. I was amazed when I saw a clip of Jackie Kennedy Onassis squeezing through crowds of reporters in front of her Fifth Avenue apartment in New York. She was on her way to board a private charter flight to Paris. The reporter announced that her husband, Aristotle Onassis, hospitalized at the International Hospital, was in serious condition. She was wrapped in a sable coat wearing her signature, large dark glasses and looked as regal and stoic as humanly possible. She arrived at the hospital later that day wearing the same coat and glasses. By then, reporters were positioned at the hospital's entrance to take pictures of her. To minimize her exposure to the press, her

Rolls Royce limousine was guarded and allowed to wait by the front door. Jackie was immediately told that her husband's condition was "critical" but that he might linger in this condition for an extended period of time before he either improved or worsened.

The prediction was curious to me as well as to several physicians who I questioned about such a prognosis. That day Jackie only stayed at the hospital a few minutes and left to go to the Onassis apartment on Avenue Foch. During the next agonizing few days, she visited her husband daily. Christina usually took a walk around the hospital gardens during Jackie's brief visits. She looked bent and weary which is no surprise because during the previous eighteen months, Christian had first lost her aunt Eugenia, then her brother and finally her mother who died the previous October at forty-five in the Niarcos mansion in Paris. The cause of that death, once-again contested, was officially determined to be from an edema of the lung and not of a drug overdose or violence as was widely reported.

I assume that when it became apparent to Jackie that her husband was stable once again, she returned to New York.

Immediately after Jackie's second departure for New York during the Onassis admission, I received a call from The Rosemort banker and member of our board in Washington.

"René," he began, "I am sure you have seen the latest figures for the company?"

"Yes," I answered hesitantly.

"Martin came in yesterday and requested additional credit as well as a third mortgage on his home. We have decided that the house is already over mortgaged and we will only give the company a small advance to hold them over until your March revenues from Paris are received. There will be no more funds from Riggs Bank."

"So, then what?" I asked sensing there was more the banker had to say.

"Our actions might well force the firm into bankruptcy. The only way we may assist you any further is if you return to Washington this month and cut the staff as well as all expenses by fifty percent on your first day back." He paused and continued: "And, incidentally, you will be Chief Executive and Martin has to retire."

My heart sank as I stood near the wall-mounted phone in the front hall of our apartment. I knew how Martin abhorred the term "retired." Somehow I was able to reply more or less coherently, "You must understand that the International Hospital revenues are critical. I will ask the Board Chairman here if he will accept Bob as my replacement and I will get right back to you."

"Okay," he said "but you have the weekend to decide and to tell Martin what is about to happen. He has to understand that this a last chance for any credit extension and he has to pass the leadership to you."

After I hung up, I explained the conversation to Delores. To my amazement she recommended that I ask Perry for a permanent position at the International Hospital and that we abandon her family and the business altogether. Delores had become both very happy with her life in Paris and with the intrigue of high society, notably my meetings with, and the resulting buzz about, the Duchess. Furthermore, she was pregnant and fearful of what life would be like back in Washington with her father being forced into retirement. I argued that worse than a forced retirement, would be a future without money.

"He is much too old to start afresh as a hospital administrator," I said. "If we can pull the company out of the nose dive with half the staff, I feel certain that we can salary him and allow your parents to have a comfortable retirement. They keep saying how they want to move back to Canada."

Eventually, Delores reluctantly agreed. With that bridge crossed, I had to see if Perry would cooperate before I placed the most difficult call of my life: to tell Martin what the bank had said and that I would be returning to Washington shortly to take the management of the company as he entered retirement. When I phoned Perry, his reaction was compassionate however he insisted on a compromise.

"You have to stay at the hospital until Onassis is discharged or, er... er... a different outcome occurs."

That "different outcome" took place during the night of March 15, 1975, the Ides of March. With his daughter, Christina, by his side, Aristotle Onassis died. He was sixty-nine years old. Jackie, accompanied by her two children, her brother-in-law, Senator Ted Kennedy, and her mother arrived from New York the same day. We had moved Onassis' body to the hospital's chapel where Jackie prayed for a few minutes and then left the building. Jackie, as expected, was composed and serene in stark contrast to Christina's Mediterranean display of emotion. Among other things, Christina complained – yelling about Jackie's "altogether too brief" praying at her father's coffin.

Doctor Chevalier made a grandiose presentation to the assembled press where he said, among other things, that Onassis'"death was due to bronchial pneumonia, which resisted all antibiotics. Mr. Onassis had been receiving cortisone treatment, which lowered the resistance to infection and made the pneumonia uncontrollable." Coincidentally, a physician and friend of Onassis who had urged the tycoon to go to

New York, Doctor Isadore Rosenfeld, was quoted as saying, "I believe that if Onassis had elected to come to New York instead of Paris, and avoid the gallbladder operation, he could have been saved." Doctor Rosenfeld had been with Onassis in Greece immediately before his friend and patient was transferred to Paris five weeks previously - in contradiction to Rosenfeld's recommendation. Had Onassis listen to Rosenfeld's sound advice, his life would in all likelihood have been extended, assuming that he had the will to live.

To underscore the real possibility that Onassis did not have that will, author Stuart Speiser concludes in his book *The Deadly Sins of Aristotle Onassis*: "If Ari had wanted to live, he would have nothing to lose by flying to New York and trying the local procedure recommended by Dr. Rosenfeld. If that failed to solve the problem, he could then have had the gallbladder removed by an eminent surgeon in New York, whom Dr. Rosenfeld had standing by." Speiser concludes that Ari's will to live had vanished as his feelings of guilt about Alexander's death increased.

In the early morning of the day Onassis died, I brought all the necessary papers to the private sitting room. Christina stayed with me and her lawyers while the documents were read and signed. An American notary had been brought to the hospital by the lawyers, as there is a different system to certify documents in France. Since I knew most of the American Embassy personnel, I assumed that the notary had been recruited elsewhere or brought over from the US. The meeting lasted nearly an hour. Christina was obviously very aware of the legal aspects of what was required and did her best to monitor the process although she was distraught beyond description. Her red eyes were sunken into her face and at times she cried aloud until her sobs ceased. She looked as if she was in shock. Before she left, I asked her if I could get her some medication to allow her to sleep and to calm her nerves. She readily accepted and the appropriate doses of medications were provided by a staff physician.

The last time I ever saw Christina was the following day when she came to my office before leaving with her father's remains to their island of Skorpios to entomb her father in a crypt adjacent to the church where many family weddings, including that of Jackie and her father, had taken place and next to Alexander's grave. She carried a handful of exorbitant physician bills that she wanted me to explain. After our discussion, the entourage, lead by Christina and Jackie, left for Skorpios and buried Onassis on March 18, 1975. As the cortege of cars drove through Athens, photographers caught pictures of Christina leaping out of her limousine and getting in one that was following hers. It is believed that she did so because she had an argument with Senator Ted Kennedy who was riding with her – possibly because he indelicately brought up the subject of a financial settlement for Jackie.

Christina would die tragically at thirty-seven, presumably from a drug overdose, in Buenos Aires thirteen years later. In the interim she married three times and divorced twice. In spite of a turbulent personal life, she had admirably handled many aspects of her late, billionaire father's foundation and shipping company. Had she lived, her only child, Athena, may well have had a more secure upbringing and the many sharks that stood ready to attack the huge but fragile foundation would not have achieved their goal.

After Christina's departure, I called Martin at his home in the Washington suburb of Potomac, Maryland to repeat what the Riggs' bank officer had told me ten days earlier. When I had finished, Martin yelled: "I'll be damned if I'll allow you and that Jew bastard at the bank to dismember my life's accomplishments, limb by limb."

"Well then, as I understand it, the only option is to shut the place down. Frankly, the situation is so dire that it may be the best option," I said sadly and only half bluffing.

"The hell with all of you," barked Martin, most probably chewing on his tie. "I will go to Guadalajara and get the biggest contract and advance we have ever had. You do whatever you like here but, you'll see, the Rosemort Group will survive! Then we can tell the bankers to go screw themselves."

My next call was to Riggs Bank. I explained Martin's position but added that I would be back in Washington after a final presentation to the Board of Governors of the International Hospital the following week. I would follow his orders to reduce all Rosemort expenses by fifty percent.

Aristotle Onassis shortly before admission
to the hospital 1975

Chapter 3

THE DUCHESS AT HER BEST

The morning of the board meeting and right after Onassis funeral, the Duchess arrived at exactly the specified time. Per her request, I was waiting for her outside the villa where the meeting was to take place. She, Genevieve, Perry and I had carefully prepared our strategy for this day and had asked Perry to arrange the Board's agenda to fit with our plan.

After kissing each other's cheeks, Wallis adopted her role as the most experienced planner. She had masterminded the show that was about to unfold and she obviously was regaling in her role.

"Now for some fun!" she exclaimed.

"Thank you for doing this, Duchess," I said, "but I hardly think it is going to be fun."

"Oh, yes it is. Just watch! You and Perry will come out on top. Poor Ari helped us by dying so conveniently!" She laughed the loud giggle that I so enjoyed and which many snobs said was not graceful.

"Genevieve has made sure Sam will be here. Is he?"

"Yes, Duchess, he is inside with everyone else – all eager to see you."

"Good," continued the Duchess. "I think Cheek and his 'pals' on the board might be a bit surprised with our team's plan. We need every ally we can get and Genevieve has prepared Sam well. She has made sure that if your, let's call it entertainment of that awful Chairman chap comes up, he will nip it in bud. Women have an ability to make their men understand certain things!" Again the Duchess laughed. "By the time we are finished with him, Cheek will have nothing to say. Honi soit qui mal y pense."

Wallis was quoting the old French motto of the most revered British knighthood and code of chivalry. The Order of the Garter, the height of British honors, is made up of some twenty august knights and headed by the Monarch and the Prince of Wales. In keeping with reminders of Edward's past, Wallis had a large embroidery of the order's gold crest with the motto which translates to "shame on those with evil thoughts."

I smiled at her sophistication and returned to my nervous concerns "I hope you are right, but both Perry and I are very anxious." Suddenly I felt selfish and self-focused. Wallis had clearly made a huge effort to plan for and attend today's meeting. I added as happily as possible: "What a stunning coat, Duchess and all Wallis blue!" She was wearing a highly tailored wool coat with pockets and a thin belt – in Wallis blue. While she looked drawn, her face lit up and she smiled which made her sapphire blue eyes sparkle.

"This talented fellow at Dior has made a few new spring things for me. I have not ordered many clothes since David died," she answered obviously pleased that I had noticed her outfit. "Look it has a matching suit!" she said with the enthusiasm of a young woman. I handed the coat to a hospital butler wearing a white jacket and standing nearby.

Clearly Genevieve's concern that Wallis may not be up to the challenge was for naught.

Wallis' hair was pulled back but not parted in the middle as the famous hairdresser, Alexandre, did for her every single evening at Le Bois when the Duke was alive. She wore a set of blue Chalcedony sapphire jewelry that had become famous because of a well-known photograph taken of her and the Duke by the renowned Canadian photographer, Karsh, only a few years earlier. Wallis liked large pieces of jewelry especially very large necklaces and this set was no exception to that rule.

"I love your necklace and earrings," I said.

"Do you know why I wore them?" she asked. "It's because Chalcedony has mystical powers. It prevents melancholy and inspires creativity. I thought we needed both today!"

The Chalcedony jewels were auctioned in different lots after the Duchess died. The necklace alone commanded $183,000 at the famous sale in Geneva. The earrings sold for $88,000, while the bracelets she had not worn that day netted $146,000. Instead of the matching bracelets, she had chosen to wear her charm bracelet for the upcoming "battle."

She laughingly explained, "And just in case we need it, I have my good luck charm bracelet which has never let me down." She held her delicate arm out for me to see it. Most pieces were engraved with special dates or loving notes from the Duke who had each object made to commemorate a unique event. "Inside this one," she continued holding a small gold locket inscribed with a date, "is a lock of David's hair, so he is here with us as well."

She carried a classic, rectangular, black leather Hermes purse. The white gold clasp had been specially made to form the interwoven

"WE" for Wallis and Edward and was attached to the handbag with a carved green jade clasp.

"Well then," she said, "let us go in. Since I do not recall meeting Deberry, please make sure I know which one he is. I should recognize our President of the Senate after all. He came to the house after the Duke died, but I was too upset to see him."

I opened the door to the boardroom and, immediately, there was a stampede of men eager to kiss the Duchess' hand; most also bowed. As soon as we had all taken our usual seats, Perry called the meeting to order and conducted the usual approval of the previous meeting's minutes and the financial statements. Then he said:

"The financial statement for the current quarter requires a special note as it is the first time the hospital has shown a profit, albeit small, that anyone can recall. I know that this has required some sacrifice but I do believe that the Rosemort Group deserves our thanks and appreciation."

A general humming of approval followed as Cheek began to speak:

"The 'sacrifice', as you call it, has been very hard on the department heads but I'd like to reserve my comments until we reach the agenda item I have requested." The item was listed at the end of the agenda as "Physician reaction to the consultant's activities."

"The next item concerns the Warnecke/Rosemort drawings for the new hospital," continued Perry, "although you have already approved the plans our new member, Mayor Deberry, representing the city and our new French advisory committee would like to comment."

Deberry thanked Perry, then acknowledged the Duchess and several members of the French nobility. He gave a description of the recent meeting of the French advisory committee and concluded: "The architects and consultants made a very thorough presentation to me and my building committee. I am pleased to tell you that – at this point – the plans conform to the city of Neuilly's building codes. I can think of no reason not to approve them when they are finalized. I would like to think that your new French advisory committee was instrumental in helping the architects interpret French morays." He shot a look in my direction that, I believe, implied "all is even now."

"Well," said Perry, "that is very good news indeed. Now let's move on to a much more distressing subject: the tragic death of Aristotle Onassis. As you all know, Mr. Onassis was treated here for the last five weeks. During this period, Mr. Silvin has been in frequent touch with Christina Onassis and would like to explain what transpired during their last discussions."

All heads turned in my direction. "Duchess, gentlemen," I began, "I'll get straight to the point. In a word we dodged the bullet." I let the words sink in before continuing. "There was no reason for Mr. Onassis to die during this admission…" The Duchess had recommended being very blunt, without any pleasantries.

"So, now you are a medical doctor?" interrupted Cheek sarcastically.

"No, doctor, I am not as we all well know, nor do I profess to be. But we need to be honest. Mr. Onassis was admitted for an autoimmune disorder of the central nervous system with a possible secondary diagnosis of gallbladder trouble. And yet he was operated on by Professor Chevalier, a general surgeon, to remove his gallbladder." I waited before continuing. "We all know that the operation was complicated by an infection, which was complicated by a likely peritonitis which was complicated by his death." Those were words Perry had had me memorize carefully.

"This is outrageous," yelled Cheek.

"Let the man continue!" exclaimed General Solberg, "I knew nothing about this. I want to hear more. Is this true?"

"It *is* true General," I said, "Christina came to my office many times during her father's stay seeking my reaction to his deteriorating condition. On her last visit, immediately before the family left Paris, two important events occurred. The first was she placed several physicians' bills on my desk and asked me if they were 'customary.' I had to explain that they were not. For example 88,000 Francs for the anesthesiologist fee during the operation was close to ten times the normal amount."

Then looking at Cheek, I continued: "I told her what to pay all the physicians concerned and suggested her attorney enclose letters saying that the attached checks were well above usual fees for comparative services at private hospitals in Europe and the amount represented 'payment in full.' She then told me that she was certain a gallbladder operation was not warranted and that her father's death was caused by the ensuing infection."

The room was so silent that one could have heard a pin drop. Instead there were only the muffled sounds of city street traffic in the distance.

"Christina went on to say," I continued, "that she had decided not to take legal action against us even though it had been recommended that she do so. I want to define what she meant by 'us'. She clearly meant the hospital and the members of the Board...."

288

"That's just a distraught daughter speaking," said Ted Williams, the US ambassador to the OECD and an IBM board member.

"Unfortunately, Mister Ambassador, it is not," I continued. "As we have discussed on several previous occasions we are an American hospital practicing medicine in France. As such, legal developments which take place in the United States apply to us. Allow me to read a recent judgment against a Mercy Hospital in Chicago as well as the individual board members, several of whom were Sisters of Mercy!"

I turned over a paper from the stack of documents in front of me and read the judge's conclusion. I had read it so many times before the meeting that I could have delivered the words from memory. Instead I chose to read for a more dramatic effect.

"'I find fault with the surgeon,'" the judgment began, "'and also with the hospital and the executive committee of the Board.'" The article concluded with, "'While it may be precedent setting to find the individual board members liable, I find them guilty of negligence.'"

"Ridiculous!" shouted Cheek again.

I continued reading with a strong voice to override his: "'... I find them guilty of negligence because the Board members knew, or at least should have known,'" I emphasized the phrase and repeated it slowly, "'or at *least should have known* that the surgeon was putting his patients at risk.'"

The people sitting around the table looked like they had seen a ghost. All except for the Duchess whose face was stoic with her eyebrows raised, feigning surprise. Perry looked at every member – one by one – to assess their reaction.

"And how is a board member supposed to know these things?" asked the Duchess looking up at the ceiling.

"The minutes of a meeting last December show that Professor Chevalier's infection rate was four times the national average in France." Several Board members uttered a gasp.

"Were any recommendations made?" asked General Solberg, as if we had also prepped him.

"I recommended we reprimand Chevalier immediately and tell him that he would no longer practice surgery at the International Hospital unless his statistics became somewhat comparable to the rest of French surgeons," I said.

"Was he summoned?" asked the Duchess well rehearsed.

"No, Duchess," I answered.

"Why not?" she continued as if she was an experienced trial attorney while all heads turned towards her in surprise that she was being so proactive.

"Doctor Cheek felt it unwise and said he would speak to the Professor and that there was no need to go any further," I said as I saw the Chief of Staff's face turn beet red.

"Is that so?" demanded Sam Prey, Genevieve's husband, looking at Perry.

"I am afraid so," Perry calmly added.

"Do you mean to tell me, that our fucking heads could roll because of this?" asked a very worried Miguel Walker, The International Bank's senior executive for Europe and the Middle East. The Duchess' expression did not change when she heard the profanity. She was used to it at these board meetings.

"Well, they won't roll this time," I began to answer, "because of what Christina also told me."

"And what was that," asked the General assuming the Duchess' role of a well-prepared defense attorney.

"Christina said that she knew we….. 'killed' was the word she used, her father. But that after discussions with Mrs. Onassis, the family advisors and their attorneys they decided that no action would be taken. The decision was reached because her father had been so miserable following her brother, Alexander's, death that he wanted to die."

"Unbelievable," said Sam, "I am shocked at what you are saying."

"It is sad, but true," I went on. "We must discuss the infection committee's report with Chevalier and demand that he come in line with national averages or lose his surgical privileges. Incidentally, it probably is a good thing that we still have no functioning tissue committee. If we had, it might reveal that there was nothing wrong with Mr. Onassis' gallbladder. And finally, I recommend we ask our lawyers at Coudert Brothers to get board member indemnity insurance protection immediately."

"I will handle it at once," said Charles Torem, a board member and senior partner of Coudert Brothers elite law firm.

"And I will call Mrs. Onassis to express our concern and appreciation. We have remained in some contact since the assassination," said Hervé Alphand, the French ambassador to Washington during the Kennedy administration.

Now the Duchess was ready to deliver her coup de grace. "Gentlemen, I believed that I was doing my bit to help the hospital by joining the Board. Perhaps this was a mistake. I had no idea that I was actually putting myself and my good name, as well as all of yours," she waved her frail arm around the table as her charm bracelet glittered, "at risk. I want to hear someone propose a motion recorded in the minutes to reflect what Mr. Silvin has said." She looked around the awestruck table of high-powered businessmen suddenly reduced to jelly.

Sam made the motion to censure Professor Chevalier which General Solberg seconded. There were no votes against the proposal. There was, however, one abstention. It was from Doctor Cheek who left the meeting before it was adjourned and before his agenda item could be raised for discussion. It never was.

I returned to Washington one week after the meeting. As I had promised the bank, I terminated half of both the professional and support staff on my first morning of my presence in the Rosemort office. All remaining employees were told their expenses had to be cut in half without exception. Martin was in Guadalajara where the University did not give the firm a contract and he never returned to the company's office. As expected, he and Miriam moved to Canada.

The International Hospital's final construction drawings were approved by the city and the actual construction, although reduced in scope, was facilitated by city officials who closed off important streets to ease the contractor's work. Homer Deberry recommended the contractor.

Chapter 4

A FAREWELL TO WALLIS

I felt it was important to properly say goodbye to my advisor and savior. She was not, as King Edward VIII had said to the British people the night of his abdication, "the woman I love" but she certainly was the woman I admired and was deeply indebted to. My first attempt to reach her was to no avail as I was told "Her Royal Highness is indisposed and resting." I called daily fearing that I would leave Paris without seeing her. Finally, when I accidently called at noon, she came to the phone and I asked if I could please drop by as soon as possible at whatever time she liked for "only a few minutes." I later learned that during this period in the Duchess' life, when her activities and visits from her friends were being curtailed by Maitre Blum, a select few friends could reach the Duchess during the lunch hour when the switchboard operator was away from her desk.

"Come by for tea tomorrow," Wallis said in a weary voice. "Le Bois at four?"

When I arrived, I was escorted into the small, casual living room that was dominated by the oxblood marble fireplace above which Wallis' famous and beautiful portrait by Gerald Brockhurst dominated the room. I assumed it was painted shortly after their wedding. Her style and posture in the painting was imposing, life-like and unforgettable. It stood in stark contrast to the diminutive figure fragilely sitting on a yellow silk antique settee. I immediately became sad and worried. As I had noticed in the past when Wallis was confused, she stared out into space and became silent rather than agitated. Our final meeting began in a way that added to the disparity between the Wallis I knew, reflected in her imposing portrait, and her current state.

In previous meetings I would never have dared to do what I instinctively did on seeing her this last time. I sat on the small couch next to her and took her hand gently in mine. She smiled broadly with an almost childlike expression begging for recognition. The Duchess was well groomed with her hair typically and immaculately pulled back into a small bun and was wearing only one piece of jewelry: her magnificent "knuckle to knuckle" emerald cut diamond solitaire. As in the past, I used an honest compliment to break her trance and begin a conversation.

"I have never seen you wear that ring, Duchess. It *is* beautiful."

There was a pause while Wallis looked at her portrait. After what seemed like an interminable silence she responded profoundly.

"I have always hated my hands," she said. "Large rings help to make them look daintier. I wore gloves long after it was no longer fashionable just to conceal them." It was not unusual for Wallis to slightly change the direction of conversations.

"I doubt you ever did anything unfashionable," I said fighting back tears.

"That is sweet, René." Again there was an extended pause as Wallis thought. "You know it is hard to understand that the chaps at the hospital think you have a wicked side. Like I was, you have been harshly criticized for doing the right thing. Do try to make such criticism strengthen you. You will always be criticized regardless of what you do, so you might as well get used to it." I assumed that similar words had been uttered to her by friends when she escaped reporters leading up to and during her six months in the South of France waiting for Edward. She sighed and added: "That was the hardest transition I ever made but was the most helpful."

A footman silently served tea using only a few phrases: "Your Royal Highness" as he handed Wallis her tea and "cream or lemon?" he asked me. He then quietly withdrew and closed the door. Wallis had trained her staff to never interrupt a conversation and to ask questions only when she paused or changed subjects.

Wallis drifted off again. It was like the brilliant strategist and fighter with whom I had spent so much time only weeks before had vanished. Could that effort have overly taxed her and hastened this condition, the worst mental absence I had witnessed to date? Was this the same soul who a few weeks before had amusingly and brilliantly said: "Poor Ari helped us by dying so conveniently!" Again I looked at her portrait and wondered what the future held in store for Wallis as we sat in silence together.

"Duchess I want to thank you for all you have done for me these last two years."

Wallis flinched as if she had received a mild electric shock and turned to look at me through her sapphire blue, yet tired, eyes.

"It was my pleasure," she began formally at first. "It gave me something interesting to do and to keep my mind off being alone in my golden cage." She laughed heartily. Then she added: "I'll probably stop going to the hospital, with you gone, there is no reason to. And

Suzanne thinks they are not worthy of my time." Wallis was referring to her attorney, Suzanne Blum, who was becoming much more influential as Wallis's mental health deteriorated.

"I'll be leaving in a few days and want you to know I will always think about you," I continued.

"Where will you be going?" she asked surprised and adding to my sadness since my imminent return to America was previously well known to her.

"Washington, Duchess, to go back to my father-in-law's company."

"I spent many happy times in Washington," she said. "But only when I was very young." Then she added pensively, "Oh no, David and I went there later. I met Mrs. Roosevelt for tea – just like this! We were also received by President and Mrs. Nixon!" Her voice picked up signaling, I knew, that she "was back."

She continued with perfect clarity and wisdom, "You'll save the company. I just know you will. It will in part be because you are so young and naïve. Regarding your wife, I have other concerns. By the time I was your age I had figured out that my first marriage was for naught. Don't wait too long." She winked and then added "I'll never forget – what's her name? - said 'backyard' instead of 'garden' and, worse, she objected to my correcting her. That was a very bad sign!"

I felt hurt for a second about her knowledge of Deloris' weaknesses and for being called "naïve." I knew she did not "approve" of Delores. Then I realized she was carefully advising me and giving me a great compliment; definitely not handing me an insult. That became completely clear with her next sentence.

"A seasoned manager would be more cautious and would better understand the risks you are about to undertake with the company and the family. Luckily you are immune and can charge ahead like a knight naively yet bravely going into battle." Again she laughed.

"I'll try, Duchess, but I won't have you to help me and to drop in to miraculously save the day," I said genuinely concerned.

"Oh yes you will. You will attract another person to protect you. It's inevitable." She reached out and touched my cheek – just for a split second. It was a flash in time but one that has stuck with me throughout the decades.

"I've often said," she continued "for a gallant spirit there can never be defeat.'" Then after a prolonged silence she said: "I shall miss you. Now go, please go. I hate goodbyes and I detest tears!" She leaned over and kissed both my cheeks and then she rang for the butler who immediately opened the doors and proceeded to tell him to see me out.

Those were the last words Wallis, Duchess of Windsor ever uttered to me. It was not, however, the last time I saw her.

A few years later, I returned to Paris for the ground breaking of the new hospital to be officiated by Homer Deberry. Perry, who also was no longer living in Paris, had warned me that Wallis' condition had "deteriorated significantly" and that he knew she was "way past being able to attend" any of the planned events. My numerous phone calls to Le Bois were all answered in the same way: "Her Royal Highness is not well" or "Her Royal Highness is not taking calls" and "I will make sure Her Royal Highness receives your message."

The night before my week long trip was to draw to an end and still not having heard Wallis' voice – a voice I would never hear again – I took a taxi to the Route du Champ d'Entrainement. The taxi driver knew exactly who lived at number 4. "Ah, Monsieur, you are going to see the home of the late Duke of Windsor."

"Yes," I said.

"There are a lot of people who ask me to take them there. They all like to look and stare hoping to see the Duchess."

As we pulled up, he said: "Look. I told you there would be tourists. They are always Americans."

The taxi stopped in front of four people who were, indeed Americans speaking to one another.

"Ya think we'll see her?" asked one lady.

"I doubt it," answered her friend, "they closed the gate when they saw us here."

I looked across the street. Even Le Bois's gate was somehow subtly different. There were no flowers. I walked around to the side of the property and climbed a small wall so I could see the mansion. I was saddened to see most of the shutters on the ground floor were closed.

"Let's go. It's no use," the other woman chimed in.

"No," said her friend. "I told Betsy in Baltimore that I would try to see her. They say she paces around upstairs and gazes out of the window all day. She doesn't know what she's looking at because she is totally out of it." Then looking at me, she asked, "Ya speak English?"

I shook my head to say "no" and threw my hands up indicating that I had no idea of what she was asking. I moved a few steps away.

"Why bother?" asked the friend. "She's nuts now anyway."

The harsh words were like a dagger in my gut. I thought of all the people who had waited to catch a glimpse of the iconic woman – *Time Magazine*'s first female "person of the year" in 1936. The word "person" was invented to replace "man" for the honor - for Wallis! I thought of the crowds hoping to see her on their many travels: on fully booked ocean liners because of their fame, during their honeymoon at their first stop in Venice where huge crowds had gathered, at big gala dinners and society events. Then everyone wanted to admire her style, her posture and jewelry. Now all they wanted was to spot someone who allegedly was "totally out of it" or even more offensive, "nuts."

I returned to my secret perch on the fence and stared at the house. Then suddenly, after only a few minutes, a small bent figure appeared beside curtains in an upstairs window. It *was* Wallis in what looked like a nightgown and, shockingly, with white hair. My throat tightened and I choked back tears. I did not wave but hoped that, at some level, Wallis knew a real friend was there – and always would be. As I walked away, I looked at the Americans, smiled, waved and said "Noblesse Oblige" as if the words meant goodbye. They did.

A grieving Duchess of Windsor at Le Bois after the Duke's funeral

1972

The Duchess of Windsor - probably her last social outing

1977

The Duchess of Windsor is laid to rest next to the Duke

April 29, 1986

On the coffin was a simple silver plate inscribed "Wallis,

Duchess of Windsor 1896-1986"

Epilogue

MEMOIRS

Both the Duke and the Duchess wrote their memoirs. The Duke's manuscript was purchased by Putman Publishing for a reported $1 million in 1947. In today's dollars it would be valued at more than ten times that amount. Since Putman obtained several copyrights for the work, it appears that it took Edward four years to complete the job – from 1947 to 1951. It is likely that the motivation for Edward to undertake the effort was to leave a record of his childhood and, importantly, his version of what happened during his affair with Wallis. I also expect the work was a result of his constant need for money. The writing of the book coincides with Edward's acquisition of The Mill, which was clearly his "replacement" for his beloved Fort Belvedere. Once he owned The Mill, he dove into his great passion for gardening which he had not enjoyed since he was King.

The couple lived a luxurious life surrounded by friends with mega fortunes. They were housed in magnificent estates staffed by large numbers of employees. However, they did not have what could be called huge wealth. When The Duke died in 1972 his total estate was three million British Pounds; roughly the equivalent of $20 million in today's terms. While any family can live very comfortably and even luxuriously with such a fortune, it does not represent wealth commensurate with their lifestyle, with the Duchess' jewels or their friends' fortunes. It was Wallis' ingenuity that managed to "stretch" their Dollars,

British Pounds and French Francs. Of all the fabulous homes they inhabited during their marriage, only one actually belonged to them: the relatively modest "Mill" outside of Paris. The other houses were all leased for very small amounts of money or loaned to the Windsors. Even many of the expenses incurred during their constant travels was either heavily subsidized or offered *gratis* in order to have one of the world's most famous couples on their ships, in their hotels and restaurants – even wearing their furs.

Edward loved to buy rare pieces of jewelry for Wallis. These were auctioned in Geneva at what was called the most successful auction of all time, a year after Wallis' death. The total receipts were reported to be $50M – considerably more than the Duke's entire estate and at more than forty times the jewels' appraised value.

In Oscar Wilde's classic comedy, *The Importance of Being Ernest,* one character says, "a man who is much talked about is always very attractive." So it was with Edward beginning with his early life, when he was adored by most of the British Empire, as well as a huge number of young women. After his marriage to Wallis, and in spite of many derogatory rumors, both he and the Duchess were "much talked about" for the rest of their lives and, as such, were also considered to be "very attractive" in social circles.

THE DUKE'S MEMOIR

A King's Story published only fifteen years after the abdication is simply dedicated "to Wallis." The above average length book begins with his birth and ends on the night of the abdication address to the British nation, his calm farewell to his brothers and his late night drive to a waiting destroyer, the Fury. There, with Wallis' Cairn terrier, Slipper, under his arm, he sailed away into the fog in the early hours of December 12, 1936. Until his memoir reaches the point of his reign that began in January, 1936, he rarely talks about Wallis and only occasionally refers to their "friendship." She is mentioned only once during his specific description of the Mediterranean cruise in 1935 which took place four years into their "friendship" and, most likely, two years after their affair began. The trip is what triggered the international press' awareness of what would become the scandal of the century – all of which is not described in Edward's book. He does acknowledge that the American press had begun to report about the lovers' trips to the continent: "I was conscious of the clouds that were rolling up on the horizon – not only clouds of war but clouds of private trouble for me; for the American press had become fascinated with my friendship for Wallis, and now pursued us everywhere."

Finally, in the fall of 1936, the British press would advise the King that their gentleman's agreement to not report any stories that touched on the personal lives of the Royal family would end. This event is what precipitated Edward's desire to clear Wallis' name and marry her. Up until that date, the closest *The London Times* had come to commenting on the King's personal life was to write, in the dawn of Edward's reign:

307

"… in the life of responsibility, day in and day out, which will henceforth be his, he will lack the help and counsel of a consort." Little did the reporter realize how strong a consort the new King already had and how far he would go to keep her. Recalling this article, which struck at the core of Edward's insecurities, Edward writes, "That sentimental sentence was to echo mutely in my ears at the end (of the abdication week) when *The Times*, once again the 'Thunderer,' turned its wrath against the woman of my choice."

Edward writes his story in two distinct parts; the first half is an interesting description of his life until the early 1930's and, the second, his life after he knew Wallis. In the first section, the reader receives a detailed and interesting view of the British monarchy as it transitioned from the Victorian era to the modern period. Edward's character and decision to abdicate played a central role in maintaining the traditional spirit of the British monarch. A role that, had he remained King, he would certainly have changed due to his dislike for formality and little respect for tradition. This trait appears numerous times in the book, beginning as early as 1913 when he reminisces "…my reactions to a party at Buckingham Palace show how little I cared for social functions…." Very shortly thereafter, when Edward went into service during World War I, he writes, "I get away from this awful place (the palace) where I have had the worst week of my life!!…" adding "What rot and a waste of time, money and energy all these state visits are."

When Edward was criticized for ignoring Royal tradition he comments, "In truth, all that I ever had in mind was to throw open the windows a little and to let into the venerable institution (the monarchy) some of the fresh air that I had become accustomed to breathe as Prince of Wales." He detested what he called "…my father's slowly turning wheel of habit…" and philosophically writes about his travels as "A rolling stone has difficulty in coming to rest."

The memoir briefly addresses Edward's views of Hitler and, therefore, the serious rumors that followed him for the rest of his life: "…I could see no point in indulging in half measures that could not succeed. It was more important in my eyes at this stage to gain an ally than to score debating victories in the tottering League of Nations." This statement is a most concise definition of "appeasement." Edward also does not mention his returning the Nazi salute on many occasions when he visited Germany, even as late as 1937 well after Edward claims he sensed "the clouds of war." Instead he chooses to soften the reader's idea that he had positive thoughts regarding Nazi Germany by describing his introductory meeting with the new German Ambassador, and Wallis' close friend, Joachim von Ribbentrop as follows, "… and there advanced toward me a tall, rigid figure in faultless tail coat and white tie. The Nazi salute with which the German Ambassador would outrage the officials of the next reign was not employed. He bowed, we shook hands…"

Both Wallis and Edward refer to their early meetings and characterize them as memorable due to her straightforwardness and atypical reprimand of the then Prince. These began with Wallis saying "but you have disappointed me Sir," referring to what she thought was a pejorative statement about American woman. Wallis had done her homework about the Prince's likes and dislikes. She delighted him in asking personal questions requiring detailed descriptions of what the job of Prince of Wales involved. This seemingly simple act was a first for Edward and one that made him feel secure and in partnership with someone. As Edward writes, "I should have been eternally grateful to Wallis for one thing: she was genuinely interested in how the Prince of

Wales went about his job. *It all began with something as simple as that*" (Italics mine). Later, when their dialogue deepened, Edward admired Wallis' ability to criticize and correct him. His words show how their characters fit, and locked, together – unable to be separated – like a stripped nut and a stripped bolt. "But most of all I admired her forthrightness. If she disagreed with one point under discussion, she never failed to advance her own views with vigor and spirit."

It was not "social functions" that Edward disliked but *Royal* social functions in general and Buckingham Palace in particular. While at the palace he felt like he was "dangling futilely in space."   After the First World War, Edward describes a conversation with his father, King George V, when his father issued one of many warnings about "proper conduct" for the Prince of Wales. "You must always remember who you are," said his father, the King. Edward then asks himself "But who exactly was I?" and he appears to have struggled with this thought until Wallis gave him a clear sense of his identity.

When Edward's sister, Mary, and later his brother, Bertie, married non Royals, Edward writes "No doubt the same dispensation would have been extended to me…" which shows how illogical and reckless Edward could be. Mary and Bertie's spouses were previously unmarried and were uncontroversial selections for a Royal. They were choices which the Cabinet, the Royal family and the Church of England could hardly find fault with. Nevertheless, the result was that Edward felt isolated, misunderstood and alone until he met Wallis. At that point, Edward could not understand the difference the Royal family felt between a twice divorced American and the choices his brother and sister had made in selecting their spouses. Describing the family gathering at Christmas in 1935, immediately before his father's death, Edward states "...I felt detached... My brothers were secure in their private lives; whereas I was caught up in an inner conflict and would have no peace of mind until I resolved it."

Edward shows himself to think and behave like a sullen child prone to emotional temper tantrums when he did not get his way. The unfortunate reality is that he could most likely have married Wallis while he was King had he listened to Winston Churchill's advice to proceed slowly and more diplomatically during his efforts to have Prime Minister Baldwin and the British Cabinet digest the concept. Importantly, Churchill advised Edward to gradually seek the opinion of his subjects and the British parliament, which was never done. Consequently, Edward's rush to find an answer to the question of marrying played directly into Baldwin's hands.

Edward, as King, had little patience to persevere with any struggle much less a battle to have Wallis accepted. Churchill's character would have welcomed a long drawn out strategic duel, but not Edward's. In the days before the abdication Edward laments "How lonely is a monarch in a struggle with a shrewd Prime Minister backed by all the apparatus of the modern state!" This account of his emotions shows the poor and incorrect view he had of himself and his lack of appreciation for the arsenal of weapons at his kingly disposal. This vulnerable sense of isolation was, in great part, caused by his hasty decision to abdicate. Once again, Wallis would breach the gap between loneliness and a sense of belonging and she would make Edward feel secure and unthreatened.

If only Edward had heeded his father's advice of "You must never speak on such controversial matters without consulting the Government." Instead, Edward presented Baldwin with a *fait accompli* with his well used phrase "marry I will!" Two days before the abdication, Edward had a rather unimportant meeting with Lincoln Ellsworth, an explorer who had just returned from the Antarctic. Still King, Edward tells a puzzled Ellsworth "Ah, to think of a whole continent with no Prime Minister, no Archbishop, no Chancellor of the Exchequer – not even a King. It must be a paradise!"

Thus, there is no doubt that Edward really wanted to leave his position as King and that Wallis gave him the perfect set of conditions to create a situation that, inevitably, would lead to the abdication. Shortly before his final decision was reached, and only a week before the abdication, Edward was walking though the garden at the Fort with his confidant and lawyer, Walter Monckton, and said, "I am beginning to wonder whether I really am the kind of King they (the Cabinet) want." He later tells Monckton, "I shall tell him (the Prime Minister) that if, as would now appear, he and the Government are against my marrying Mrs. Simpson I am prepared to go." Monckton was dumbstruck to hear these words from his King.

Like many people in very important positions, Edward was "thin skinned" and susceptible to criticism. Therefore he took the battle to achieve an unreasonable request (have the still-married Wallis accepted as his future wife) personally. Speaking of his "enemies," characterized by Prime Minister Baldwin, "... they had clearly misjudged their man. I was obviously in love. They had struck at the very roots of my pride." This deep personal hurt caused the events during the week that preceded the abdication to escalate rapidly which, once again, worked against Edward as he backed himself into a corner. With each turn of the escalating battle with Baldwin, Edward became more rushed and more stubborn. Had the two parties respected each other, there may well have been room for compromise but this was not the case. The roots of the mutual distrust were deep and there is ample evidence that Edward disliked Baldwin as early as during Baldwin's second term when he and the Prince traveled together. It annoyed Baldwin greatly that Edward gave him no credit for his many accomplishments. One must remember that Stanley Baldwin served as British Prime Minister three times. On one occasion he was appointed Prime Minister (over Lord Curzon) by Edward's father, King George V, until elections could be held.

Baldwin certainly felt Edward's disdain for him, which did not motivate the Prime Minister to come to the aid of what he thought, was an ungrateful, spoiled man. In return, Edward never gave Baldwin credit for his service as head of the Conservative Party nor did he acknowledge that his father, King George V, had made Stanley Baldwin the Earl of Bewdly. Instead Edward ridiculed Baldwin's appearance and odd mannerisms – even his "motor" (his car). In all, this was a duo that could not cooperate and solve problems due to a considerable mutual lack of respect.

Baldwin pressed Edward for an "immediate decision" regarding abdication and thwarted Edward's various attempts to "find a solution," to use Wallis' words. During that fateful last week of Edward's brief reign, Baldwin managed to engineer the British Dominions' rejection of the idea of marriage; he denied Edward the concept of the morganatic marriage, and even Edward's request to address the nation to solicit his subjects' support which, much to Baldwin's concern, later began on its own in the streets of London. Finally, when it was too late to continue the battle, Edward asked Baldwin to allow Wallis' divorce to become effective immediately upon his abdication. By now the fight had become so personal that Baldwin, rather cruelly, denied the King this very simple request. Therefore Edward was forced to stay in exile in Austria until Wallis' divorce became final. Although these miserable months at Baron de Rothschild's castle were the loneliest of Edward's life, he never regretted his decision and counted the days until he could meet and marry Wallis. Perhaps because it was so sad, this period is not discussed in Edward's memoir.

Edward needed, and found, escapes throughout his life. First, he was able to have his own existence – separate from the family – through his globetrotting. Second, his relative solitude at the Fort. Finally, his self-imposed exile with Wallis. An exit from Royal life is what he wanted and what he managed to achieve. Early on, the escapes were symbolic (travel and his love to fly in his own airplane) but later the exit needed to be final and deliberate. Even his closest friends did not understand this. In what Edward called "a plot within a plot," Edward's allies begged Wallis to leave Edward during his final days as King. The well-meaning friends felt that if Wallis broke off the relationship, Edward would remain on the throne. Quite to the contrary, when Wallis did in fact sincerely offer to "withdraw," which was spread to the public in a news release from Cannes, France, Edward made the final decision to sign the abdication papers. Edward describes this last gasp effort to keep him on the throne as "the conspiracy that failed." This phrase shows beyond any doubt that, in the King's mind, anyone eager to keep him on the throne was the enemy.

The closing words of the book are "…I today draw comfort from the knowledge that time has long sanctified a true and faithful union."

There would be twenty-one more years, until his death, to further "sanctify a faithful union." So, when all is said and done, one must conclude that, given Edward's character, he had a better life as the socialite Duke of Windsor with Wallis than as King of England without her; where he would have been bound by tradition. In stark contrast to his behavior prior to his marriage, his life with Wallis gave him a feeling of belonging, stability and consistency with a single partner. The Duke's last days and eventual death, surrounded by his personal items, competent nurses, his dog and his beloved Wallis was enviable. If only the Duchess could have experienced a similar end.

Cover of Life Magazine

May, 1950

Featuring the Duke's autobiography

A King's Story

THE DUCHESS' MEMOIR

The Heart Has It's Reason was self-published by The Duchess in 1956. The title is part of a famous quote from the 17th century French romantic philosopher, Blaise Pascal (1623-1662). The full quote is "the heart has its reason that reason does not know." It is often referred to as a justification for irrational behavior caused by a great love. It could not have been a more clever or appropriate title for either the Duke or the Duchess' memoir. Like the Duchess, Pascal was widely respected by some, notably for his romantic ideas, and despised by others (due to his theories on the irrationality of believing in God). Although Pascal is not ever mentioned by name in the work, the Duchess' choice of title and philosopher is a perfect metaphor for her life. Underscoring the synchronicity of their lives, there is a chapter in the Duke's memoir also entitled *The Heart Has It's Reason*, but Wallis does not disclose this small yet informative fact in her book. Like The Duke's memoir, hers is dedicated to him and also simply says "To David."

Memoirs, by definition, are a description of one's personal recollection of their experiences. It has been said that there is some truth in all fiction and some fiction in all truth. *The Heart Has Its Reason* offers the reader many interesting facts about Wallis' life, from birth until the time of the book's publication. It also rapidly glosses over the various scandals that surrounded her and gives her own somewhat distorted views of other events. Several aspects of her controversial life are totally omitted while admirable experiences are expanded upon. In her defense, however, she never mentions the important distinction she received in 1936 when *Time Magazine* featured her, the first woman ever, to become "Person of the Year." As was appropriate for the period, and mirroring the Duke's book, there is absolutely no mention, much less description, of anything remotely sexual.

Obviously, it was written in an era before the existence of computers or even primitive word processors, which means that the project was an exhaustive and time-consuming effort. As was, and is, the case with famous people's memoirs, Wallis must have had significant assistance from one or more "ghost writers." There are at least two distinctly different professional writing styles in *The Heart Has Its Reason*, which would imply that more than one writer, worked with the Duchess. There are also a few poorly written – but very revealing – sections which were likely written by Wallis who must have forbidden any editing.

The Duchess is not accurate about the year, and more importantly the circumstances of her birth. Also her account of her illness when she left China that, all authorities describe as a serious infection following a probable self-induced abortion, is brief and likely inexact. More amusing are her versions of the various problems that led to her two divorces, first from a most likely drunken bisexual (Win Spenser) and, later, from Ernest Simpson. She had already become Prince Edward's mistress and had to accuse Simpson of infidelity in order to file for divorce.

Her description of meeting the Prince of Wales not only differs from most historians but also from the Duke's own memory. The Duke affectionately accused Wallis of being "without documentation" which, in his definition, meant she kept no records. Wallis did not save letters, newspapers or other pieces of information; this is in stark contrast to The Duke's habits, a subtle difference that is indicative of their respective educations and his love of facts. Fortunately for history's sake,

Wallis' beloved Aunt Bessie Merryman kept the abundant amount of correspondence from her niece. Since Bessie frequently visited Wallis and, later, spent time with both Wallis and Edward, she was a huge source of information when Wallis' memoir was written. Then in her 90's, Bessie was still very clear-minded and directly involved in the project. Aunt Bessie died in November 1964, at the age of 100.

Not surprisingly, Wallis' account of how Thelma's, Lady Furness', affair with the Prince ended is quite dissimilar to everyone else's. In the memoir, Wallis says "something had happened between her (Thelma) and the Prince." She does not explain that the "something" was Wallis had become the Prince's lover during Thelma's prolonged visit to the United States. There is no mention of when Wallis' status as Royal mistress actually began. In fact, her memoir, through the omission of when they became lovers, implies that sex may never have been the central issue.

Her detailed description about the escape from England on the eve of the King's abdication is riveting and, most assuredly, perfectly accurate. She is generous in her thoughts about her hosts in France, Katherine and Herman Rogers, even though her letters indicated that there was some friction due to Wallis being uncomfortable at the villa, Lou Viei, during the cold winter months. She does give Herman the respect he is due in his unending assistance as well as his prediction of Wallis' future: "Whether you like it or not, he said to me one day, the world is discovering you....you'd better learn to live with these things." In similar statements, quoted by Wallis, Herman was preparing Wallis to live a life of great comfort and fame as well as one that would always be scrutinized by the press. This was new to Wallis given the heretofore "gentleman's agreement" with the British press not to discuss the King's private life.

Her account of the wedding itself also differs from historians' only as it relates to the difficulty of identifying who would marry them and what credentials that person would possess. The reason behind these problems, her lack of a birth record and the roadblocks set in place by the Royal family and the Church of England, are omitted.

To her credit, the work honors and reveres her beloved David. She manages to lovingly describe and justify his occasional bad temper and his often-excessive demands for creature comforts. She describes herself as a wife who provides her husband with all his needs, which is probably more true than Wallis discusses. She offers the reader a view of the Duke as a gentle, protective, forgiving, generous and loving man.

Finally, the description of their tenure in the Bahamas is somewhat of a "whitewash." The reader is led to believe that they single handedly solved all the local problems caused by poverty and war, that they were happy with the official accommodations, rarely left their duties and became true civil servants who were in demand by Presidents and policy makers. Once again, a memoir is the author's view of the truth. She admits that their mission during the war was an "ambiguous and amorphous position" which she asserts they handled most admirably because they had "none of the advantages of royalty and all of its disadvantages." All the while, their inner thoughts were remnants of colonialism within a world that had changed.

We must remember the huge difference in women's roles during the twentieth century; Wallis' century. She was most assuredly a bright, strong and cerebral woman when, sadly, it was neither popular nor acceptable for a lady to be so. The last chapter of her memoir expands upon and justifies this dilemma as follows:

"Quite apart from other differences, women seem to me to be divided into two groups – those who reason and those who are for-ever casting about for reasons for their own lack of reason. While I might wish it to be the contrary, the record of my life, now that I have for the first time attempted to see it as a whole, clearly places me with the second group. Women, by and large, I have concluded, were never meant for plan and planning."

This convoluted, poorly written, close to her book was assuredly written by Wallis. It evokes many of the paradoxes of her life. Clearly Wallis *did* plan, reason and was, in fact, a master of doing so in a way that even the King of England found acceptable and endearing. To her credit, she was both a survivor and a fighter; she knew when and how to play each role. This was a character trait that the British Royal family despised in her and did not accept in any Royal women. Wallis' story is undeniably one of a lady with great style, intelligence, ambi-tion and, to those dear to her: generosity. She was also self-indulgent, capable of carrying strong bitterness (which she escalated into ven-dettas) and held animosity over long periods of time. All these traits came together to assist me, a young man wrongly accused, in her mind, of being a "young upstart."

In 1974, Lord Louis Mountbatten, who had been a close friend of both Wallis and the Duke, as well as a loyal member of the Royal fam-ily, requested that Wallis donate many of the Duke's personal items to be preserved at Buckingham Palace and various museums. I was close to Wallis during this period and knew she considered the request very seriously and over a span of several months. Finally, the appeal was largely denied, most likely influenced by Wallis' attorney, Suzanne Blum, who, once in charge of these items after Wallis died, organized the most successful auction of all time. It was held at the Beau Rivage hotel in Geneva, Switzerland in April of 1987. To the huge disappointment of the powers at the International Hospital, it received none of the estimated $50 million in proceeds from the auction. Instead the total amount went to the Pasteur Institute with much of it specifically earmarked for AIDS research. This change is particularly ironic because Edward was often overly critical of homosexuality and yet the residual of his estate went to AIDS research at Pasteur: an illness that, in those days, was considered a "gay curse." As a footnote to prove how famous and revered the couple was, the total proceeds from the auction surpassed Edward's and Wallis' combined estates at the time of their deaths.

Maitre Suzanne Blum deserves a postscript to this story. Like Wallis she was heavily criticized. Unlike the Duchess whose reputation is improving over time, that of Suzanne Blum is not. The reason, in part, is that Maitre Blum gradually took complete control of Wallis' life and directed the disposal of her estate. One must remember that Wallis' mental health deteriorated significantly and rapidly in the late 1970's. From 1980 until her death on April 24, 1986 Wallis never left Le Bois, other than for hospitalization. She lost control of her hands and legs and had to be assisted with all her bodily needs. Understandably, Suzanne Blum gradually reduced the staff from fifteen to a "just" six: one maid, a butler a gardener and three nurses to assure around the clock coverage of their ward. It is unclear why Maitre Blum tried to isolate the ailing Duchess from the few friends who repeatedly tried to visit the bedridden Duchess. Her motives will forever be a subject of debate with an increasing number of authorities – including myself – questioning the attorney's integrity.

Many people condemned Maitre Blum for the superficial cutbacks as well as the gradual elimination of the army of beauticians and estheticians who previously had regularly scheduled appointments at the house. During her final, six-year confinement at Le Bois, Wallis' hair was white and she was either confined to her wheelchair or bed. But she was cared for at home and allowed to live in this stricken state until her heart simply stopped beating on its own. In today's way of looking at these events a more "humane" end might be the still-controversial decision to discontinue life support. But who, in Wallis' case, could have taken that decision? It can be argued that the British Royals were the Duchess' next of kin. Obviously, Queen Elizabeth could never have subjected herself to the outrage that would have followed such a move. Unfortunately, the Duchess had no human heirs or close family to take any initiative on the subject. The shocking result was the poor, tortured lady endured more than five years of being bedridden, further dehumanized on a nasal feeding tube with her hands bound apparently for her security. Such prolonged, inhumane treatment would be aborted long before any "ordinary" patient's heart stopped beating on its own five years hence. Ironically, however, such obvious and common decency was denied the Duchess.

Most dog lovers believe strongly in a canine's affectionate ability to soothe an ailing owner. To those people it is further distressing to learn that the Duchess' loving pugs were not allowed to stay close to their mistress. While not mistreated they were relegated to a separate building on the estate, allegedly for "sanitary reasons."

Maitre Blum, who was only two years younger than Wallis and suffered health issues of her own, undertook the all-encompassing effort to supervise Le Bois and the Duchess. To her credit she never made disrespectful comments or offered dehumanizing details to the numerous friends who, in the early years of Wallis' dementia, called frequently. This is in contrast to the chief of staff of the International Hospital who made a house call every week. He indelicately, repeatedly and publicly referred to the Duchess as "a complete vegetable." However, two lingering, pertinent questions about Maitre Blum's integrity remain. Specifically, when and under what circumstances was the Duchess' last will and testament altered and why were friends and dignitaries not allowed to visit the Duchess once she was allegedly unable to take phone calls?

Luckily Wallis was relatively well treated by both Queen Elizabeth and even the Queen mother toward the end of her coherent life. Her Majesty, Queen Elizabeth, was magnanimous in allowing Wallis to be buried at Frogmore and to be treated as a member of the family during the Duke's funeral. She visited the Duke and Duchess in 1972, only five days before her uncle died. The Queen mother, also named Elizabeth, tried to see Wallis in Paris in 1976. The proposed meeting was cancelled probably by Suzanne Blum stating "ill health." Nevertheless, the Queen mother sent flowers and a note simply saying, "In Friendship. Elizabeth."

While Wallis never saw David's mother, Queen Mary, after the abdication, Queen Mary did close some of her letters to her son with "please give my regards to your wife." And Wallis truly was Edward's *wife* – in the very best sense of the word. They were partners that survived the test of time and, even if it is hard to grasp, they survived great adversity and temptations. Seen with the wisdom only acquired with the passing of time, what really counts is that no matter what Wallis had said or done or been, in the end, Edward was all that really mattered to her.

How one behaves *vis a vis* one's life partner during good times is of, of course, interesting. However, it is how one behaves during crisis and illnesses which truly define a partner's devotion, love and commitment. From the onset of the Duke's declining health, Wallis was totally dedicated to caring for her husband to the best of her ability. Once the Duke's condition became serious, she rarely left his side and fought to protect his dignity while she continued to provide him with as much comfort and affection as possible. After the Duke' death, and rather like a swan, the tragedy and solitude was impossible for Wallis to overcome. Although unlikely, losing her conscious mind and retreating into the depths of her psyche, hopefully focusing on pleasant memories, was, I'd like to romanticize, a welcome salvation to her loneliness.

In her philosophical treatise on women, the very last paragraph of her memoir, Wallis states:

"Any woman who has been loved as I have been loved, and who, too, has loved, has experienced life in its fullest. To this I must add one qualification, one continuing regret. I have never known the joy of having children of my own. Perhaps no woman can say her life has been completely fulfilled unless she has had a part in the miracle of creation."

Possibly her fierce, energetic defense of me and my relatively insignificant efforts at the International Hospital of Paris was because she had focused on that "one continuing regret," during the two years when I, only in my late twenties, saw a great deal of her. Also, after

Edward died, Wallis had no taste or energy for personal scandals or rumors. The few public appearances she made had to be with an unthreatening escort and, fortunately, I fit that description. If both of these suppositions are true, how fortunate I was to be so viewed by this amazing figure during her final years with mental clarity and physical energy.

One can only quote the motto of Edward VIII's Order of the Garter when one hears many people exaggerate her flaws, invent scandalous stories, fail to consider her many talents and speak disrespectfully of the Duchess during her tragic senile years: Honi soit qui mal y pense.

Shame to those with evil thoughts.

The Duchess of Windsor, late 1940's

Wearing a pearl necklace and pendant that had belonged to Queen Mary

and was later bought by Calvin Klein

BIBLIOGRAPHY

A King's Story, The Memoirs of the Duke of Windsor, by Edward, Duke of Windsor

Architectural Digest, December 1991, "Fort Belvedere, Inside the Private Realm of Edward VIII and Wallis Simpson"

Behind Closed Doors, The Tragic, Untold Story of the Duchess of Windsor, by Hugo Vickers

Churchill, Hitler and the Unnecessary War by Patrick J. Buchanan

Crowning Glory, American Wives of Princes and Dukes, by Richard Jay Hutto

Duchess of Windsor, The Uncommon Life of Wallis Simpson by Greg King

Flair, The Paris House of the Duke and Duchess of Windsor by Margaret Biddle

Stars Aboard, Celebrities of yesteryear who traveled Cunard Line during the golden age of transatlantic travel by Cunard Line.

The Deadly Sins of Aristotle Onassis by Stuart M. Speiser

The Duke and Duchess of Windsor, The Private Collection, Sotheby's

The Duke and Duchess of Windsor, The Public Collection, Sotheby's

The Duchess of Windsor, The Secret Life by Charles Higham

The Heart Has Its Reason by Wallis, Duchess of Windsor

The Jewels of the Duchess of Windsor, by Sotheby's Vendome Press

Noblesse Oblige

<u>The Private World of the Duke and Duchess of Windsor</u>, by Hugo Vickers

<u>The Windsor Style</u> by Suzy Menkes

<u>The Woman He Loved</u> by Ralph G. Martin

<u>Picture History of the SS United States</u> by William H. Miller, Jr.

<u>Picture History of the Andrea Doria</u> by William H. Miller, Jr.

ABOUT THE AUTHOR

Born in New York, Richard René Silvin grew up in Swiss boarding schools from ages seven through eighteen. After earning his Bachelor's degree from Georgetown University in 1970 and an MBA in both Hospital Administration and Finance from Cornell University in 1972, he spent twenty-five years in the hospital industry.

Upon graduation, he joined his father-in-law's hospital consulting firm where he founded the American Academy of Hospital Consultants and quickly became President of the small struggling company which he sold to American Medical International (NYSE: AMI) in 1976.

Following an administrative collapse at a famous American hospital in Paris in 1973, Silvin's firm was hired by USAID to become that hospital's interim crisis Executive Director. Living in Paris he worked with the recently widowed Duchess of Windsor, who served on the

331

hospital's Board of Governors which was the then-lonely duchess' only charity and passion. She partnered with Silvin on a mission to restore the hospital, its management and medical staff to its former greatness. She taught Silvin how to wage a high-stake political battle against the establishment while enlisting the support of key players in Paris' highly social Franco-American community and she treated him as the son she never had.

Silvin eventually rose to head the International Division of AMI which owned and operated thirty hospitals in nine countries. He was listed in *Who's Who in Health Care, Who's Who in Finance and Industry and Who's Who in the World*. He lectured at numerous graduate schools of hospital administration at universities in the United States and Europe.

Noblesse Oblige – a work inspired by a true story — is Silvin's third autobiographical book, including *I Survived Swiss Boarding Schools* and *Walking the Rainbow*. He lives in West Palm Beach, Florida, and Highlands, North Carolina.

Made in the USA
Charleston, SC
18 October 2011